THE GREENHAVEN PRESS COMPANION TO
Literary Movements and Genres

Postmodernism

Derek Maus, *Book Editor*

Bonnie Szumski, *Editorial Director*

Scott Barbour, *Managing Editor*

David M. Haugen, *Series Editor*

Greenhaven Press, Inc., San Diego, CA

Every effort has been made to trace the owners of copyrighted material. The articles in this volume may have been edited for content, length, and/or reading level. The titles have been changed to enhance the editorial purpose. Those interested in locating the original source will find the complete citation on the first page of each article.

Library of Congress Cataloging-in-Publication Data

Postmodernism / Derek Maus, book editor.
        p.   cm. — (The Greenhaven Press companion to literary movements and genres)
    Includes bibliographical references and index.
    ISBN 0-7377-0640-6 (pbk. : alk. paper) —
ISBN 0-7377-0641-4 (lib. bdg. : alk. paper)
    1. Postmodernism (Literature) I. Maus, Derek. C. II. Series.

PN98.P67 P673 2001
809'.9113—dc21   00-065398
                                                      CIP

Cover photo: Kactus Foto, Santiago, Chile/SuperStock

Copyright © 2001 by Greenhaven Press, Inc.
PO Box 289009
San Diego, CA 92198-9009
Printed in the U.S.A.

CONTENTS

Chapter 1: Understanding Postmodernism

1. The New Understanding of Language
by Italo Calvino   28

As the understanding of how language works grows, so do
the possibilities for innovative forms of literary expression
based on that understanding. When humans are capable of
creating a machine that can write literature, will its style
be the ultimate form of postmodernism?

2. Ten Points About Postmodernism *by Ihab Hassan*   36

Postmodernism originally arose as a challenge to the status quo in the field of literary criticism. As postmodernism
has become an established school of thought itself, several
questions about its nature and meaning need to be clarified in order to apply it as an organizing principle to
works of literature.

3. Irony as the Defining Principle of Postmodernism
by Umberto Eco   43

Postmodernism consists largely of an ironic response to
the past, one which playfully acknowledges both the
meaning of a particular piece of writing and the self-aware
knowledge that this meaning is not original.

4. Postmodernism and the Art of Writing
by Donald Barthelme   49

Using the beginning of a story as both an example and as a
disguise for an essay on the difficulties of writing, one of
postmodernism's most representative authors presents a
means for understanding the composition process of his
own fiction.

Chapter 2: Types of Postmodernism

1. The Tragic View of Categories *by John Barth*   57

Like so many of the phrases that have come before, postmodernism is an inherently insubstantial description for a

class of literary works. Even one of the writers who is most frequently associated with it claims that it is difficult for him to understand what makes his work postmodernist after twenty years of trying to do so.

Chapter 3: Postmodern Writers and Their Works

is wholly separate from that of the "real" one. In this way, the author challenges conventional notions of free will and morality by reinventing the world as a less terrifying place.

Chapter 4: Criticisms of Postmodern Theory

FOREWORD

The study of literature most often involves focusing on an individual work and uncovering its themes, stylistic conventions, and historical relevance. It is also enlightening to examine multiple works by a single author, identifying similarities and differences among texts and tracing the author's development as an artist.

While the study of individual works and authors is instructive, however, examining groups of authors who shared certain cultural or historical experiences adds a further richness to the study of literature. By focusing on literary movements and genres, readers gain a greater appreciation of influence of historical events and social circumstances on the development of particular literary forms and themes. For example, in the early twentieth century, rapid technological and industrial advances, mass urban migration, World War I, and other events contributed to the emergence of a movement known as American modernism. The dramatic social changes, and the uncertainty they created, were reflected in an increased use of free verse in poetry, the stream-of-consciousness technique in fiction, and a general sense of historical discontinuity and crisis of faith in most of the literature of the era. By focusing on these commonalities, readers attain a more comprehensive picture of the complex interplay of social, economic, political, aesthetic, and philosophical forces and ideas that create the tenor of any era. In the nineteenth-century American romanticism movement, for example, authors shared many ideas concerning the preeminence of the self-reliant individual, the infusion of nature with spiritual significance, and the potential of persons to achieve transcendence via communion with nature. However, despite their commonalities, American romantics often differed significantly in their thematic and stylistic approaches. Walt Whitman celebrated the communal nature of America's open democratic society, while Ralph Waldo

Emerson expressed the need for individuals to pursue their own fulfillment regardless of their fellow citizens. Herman Melville wrote novels in a largely naturalistic style whereas Nathaniel Hawthorne's novels were gothic and allegorical.

Another valuable reason to investigate literary movements and genres lies in their potential to clarify the process of literary evolution. By examining groups of authors, literary trends across time become evident. The reader learns, for instance, how English romanticism was transformed as it crossed the Atlantic to America. The poetry of Lord Byron, William Wordsworth, and John Keats celebrated the restorative potential of rural scenes. The American romantics, writing later in the century, shared their English counterparts' faith in nature; but American authors were more likely to present an ambiguous view of nature as a source of liberation as well as the dwelling place of personal demons. The whale in Melville's *Moby-Dick* and the forests in Hawthorne's novels and stories bear little resemblance to the benign pastoral scenes in Wordsworth's lyric poems.

Each volume in Greenhaven Press's Companions to Literary Movements and Genres series begins with an introductory essay that places the topic in a historical and literary context. The essays that follow are carefully chosen and edited for ease of comprehension. These essays are arranged into clearly defined chapters that are outlined in a concise annotated table of contents. Finally, a thorough chronology maps out crucial literary milestones of the movement or genre as well as significant social and historical events. Readers will benefit from the structure and coherence that these features lend to material that is often challenging. With Greenhaven's Literary Movements and Genres in hand, readers will be better able to comprehend and appreciate the major literary works and their impact on society.

INTRODUCTION

The word *postmodernism* seems to contain a pair of troubling logical contradictions. If "modern" means both "contemporary" and "enlightened," how can a philosophy exist currently that, by its very name, claims to exist *after* the present? Furthermore, the prefix *post-* also implies that the "modern" has been completed; doesn't this suggest that postmodernism is a way of thinking that admits to being unenlightened, thus denying its own potential truth?

The reality of postmodernism is only somewhat different from this confusing linguistic logic. It is a response to the "modern" not in the everyday usage of the word, but rather in its artistic definition. "Modernism" is closely associated with a set of cultural and artistic values dating back to the first half of the twentieth century. As such, postmodernism is generally considered to be the direct offspring of modernism as well as its adversary. As the second half of the century progressed, a number of different social and artistic movements began to refer to themselves or be referred to by others (willingly or unwillingly) as postmodernist because of their notable departure from established standards.

Despite the frequency with which the word has been used—appearing everywhere from the nightly news and political campaigns to college classrooms and movie reviews—its widespread acceptance as a way of thinking is far from complete. Perhaps because of its strong political tendencies and perhaps because of its adaptability to a wide variety of literary and artistic styles, postmodernism has often been attacked as an empty philosophy, whose goal is simply to invalidate time-honored beliefs without offering any suitable replacement.

The goal of this volume is not necessarily to defend postmodernism from such criticism, but to present a wide range of different voices affiliated in some way with postmodernism and consider what they have to say about it. From innovative writers discussing their own techniques, to authors singing the praises of their colleagues' work, and from literary critics analyzing fiction using unusual and complex new methods, to skeptics claiming that these methods are based on faulty foundations, this volume contains a diverse sampling of ideas that explicitly or implicitly deal with the messy concept that is postmodernism.

One may wonder, of course, why anyone would want to contend with such an ill-defined concept. The best answer to this question comes from Kathy Acker, herself a major postmodernist. In describing why she believes postmodernism is a valuable philosophy, Acker argues that language is a tool, often the only tool, that is available to otherwise powerless segments of society. Whereas modernism had once served a useful purpose in questioning the basis of Western culture in the wake of World War I, it had largely been absorbed by society by the late 1940s. Hence, postmodernism became the means by which writers could criticize elements of the status quo in their art. Acker writes, "In such a society as ours the only possible chance for change, for mobility, for political, economic, and moral flow lies in the tactics of guerrilla warfare, in the use of fictions, of language." The views collected in this volume will allow you to experience some of these criticisms for yourself and decide whether or not postmodernism is, as Acker calls it, "a useful perspective and tactic" for making sense of the world of the last fifty years.

POSTMODERNISM: AN OVERVIEW

Postmodernism is a term with seemingly as many definitions as there are definers. To some, it is a broadly defined philosophical concept that describes a skeptical cultural reaction to such monumental historical events as World War II, the Holocaust, and the nuclear arms race. To others, postmodernism is a purely artistic movement that arose in response to the modernist sensibility that predominated in the first half of the twentieth century. Still others claim that postmodernism is a way of thinking that blends science and art, thus combining ideas that had previously been considered inherently separate. Finally, some extreme theorists of postmodernism (and many of its harshest critics) conceive of it as a philosophy that rejects absolutes of any kind, including good and evil, truth and falsehood, history and fiction. No single definition of postmodernism has become the clearly accepted standard, a problem that has caused considerable anxiety among writers such as John Barth, whose works are regularly cited as prime examples of postmodern literature. Barth and others like him have openly questioned whether or not a work of art can be usefully classified as postmodernist if the theoreticians of the philosophy cannot even agree on its basic characteristics.

While it is beyond both the scope and the intention of this book to settle this debate, it is important that a reader approaching postmodernism for the first time gain some familiarity with the more compelling definitions of postmodernism, particularly those explicitly concerned with the study of literature. The essays included in this volume comprise a broad sampling of practical applications of postmodernist ideas to the production of literature. Advanced theoretical and philosophical essays have been avoided, both because of their innate complexity and because of their tendency to rely on the highly specialized language of literary criticism, which makes them rather inaccessible to readers not extensively trained in analyzing literature. Postmodernism as a literary phenomenon is somewhat unusual in that it is derived as much from philosophical theorists as from artists and writers. While neither group is particularly more "right" or "wrong" concerning the meaning of postmodernism, the selections in this volume give considerably more attention to artistic works of postmodernism (and to the perspectives of the writers who produce them) than to the critical theories that supposedly frame such works. Nevertheless, a brief summary of the historical development of postmodernism as a critical term—with special focus on some of its most prominent theorists—is necessary to establish the context in which the debate over this slippery term's usage has raged.

THE BIRTH OF POSTMODERNISM

The coinage of the term *postmodernism* is generally attributed to Federico de Onís, a Spanish literary critic of the 1930s. In the introduction to an anthology of poetry published in 1934, he used the word *postmodernismo* in reference to a school of Spanish-language poets who were producing work that contrasted significantly with the modernist style that prevailed not only in Spain, but in England, America, and most of western Europe. *Postmodernism* was first used in English by the distinguished British historian Arnold Toynbee in describing the historical period following the Franco-Prussian War, which ended in 1871. As Perry Anderson writes:

> "Western communities became 'modern'" [Toynbee] wrote, "just as soon as they had succeeded in producing a bourgeoisie [middle class] that was both numerous enough and competent enough to become the predominant element in society." By contrast, in the postmodern age this middle class was no longer in the saddle. Toynbee was less definitive about what followed. But certainly the postmodern age was marked by two developments: the rise of an industrial working class in the West, and the bid of successive intelligentsias outside the West to master the secrets of modernity and turn them against the West.[1]

Toynbee's sociohistorical usage differs considerably from its usage in literary history, in which modernism was a stylistic and thematic phenomenon confined largely to the first half of the twentieth century. Contemporary definitions of postmodernism combine de Onís's idea of postmodernism as án artistic reaction to modernism and Toynbee's concept of postmodernism as a historical period that logically follows modernism (as the prefix *post-* implies).

During the 1910s, '20s, and '30s, writers such as Ezra Pound, Ernest Hemingway, Virginia Woolf, James Joyce, W.B. Yeats, Franz Kafka, D.H. Lawrence, T.S. Eliot, F. Scott Fitzgerald, Rainer Maria Rilke, Gertrude Stein, and William Faulkner popularized a form of writing that became known as modernism, a movement that also found vigorous expression in architecture (Frank Lloyd Wright), painting (Pablo Picasso), and music (Igor Stravinsky). Modernism as an artistic attitude developed no distinct manifesto, but the authors who came to be associated with it shared a number of thematic and stylistic similarities that have served to define the term for subsequent critical usage.

Modernism was perceived as a radical break from the past, both in terms of artistic expression and often in politics. World War I was culturally and personally traumatic for a number of the most prominent modernist writers and their works often reflect bitter irony and a sense of lost innocence. The modernists broke with "old" traditions like Victorianism and created a new art that they felt more accurately reflected the altered and pessimistic state of the post–WWI Western world. While the specific ways in which modernism sought to "make it new" (Pound's often-quoted rallying cry to his fellow modernist writers) varied, a number of themes and techniques recur with great enough frequency to characterize the movement as a whole: symbolic associations with archetypal themes (derived from patterns or models that reappear throughout a particular culture's history), especially those derived from folklore and/or mythology; an ironic pessimism toward humanity's potential for goodness; an emphasis on personal reason over tradition (or, in political terms, democracy over monarchy); individualism that asserts the natural rights of women and members of other traditionally subjugated groups; a solemn sense of seriousness; notable self-consciousness and a search for higher truths through psychological insight; a preference for abstract or at least impressionistic depictions over strictly realistic ones.

Postmodern literature generally builds on a number of these modernist characteristics, although the work of the authors most closely associated with postmodernism also tends to exaggerate or otherwise modify modernist philosophies before using them. The editors of *Postmodern American Fiction: A Norton Anthology* identify the following concepts (some of which are direct echoes of modernism) as central to postmodernism:

- an assault upon traditional definitions of narrative . . . particularly those that created coherence or closure
- the theme of the suburbanization of America, the decline of the city, and apocalyptic visions of the devastated city
- fascination about how the public life of the nation intersects with the private lives of its citizens
- questioning of any belief system that claims universality or transcendence (the ability to surpass the boundaries of human comprehension)
- the proliferation of the nonfiction novel [e.g., Tom Wolfe's *The Electric Kool-Aid Acid Test* (1968) or Hunter S. Thompson's *Fear and Loathing in Las Vegas* (1971)], a genre that "extends the experiments of the New Journalism and further undermines the distinctions between journalism and literature, fact and fiction"
- the creation of "ruptures, gaps, and ironies that continually remind the reader that an author is present" and which demonstrate "how individuals use fictional constructions to make order of real-life events."[2]

C. Hugh Holman and William Harmon further define the differences between modernism and postmodernism:

The fundamental philosophical assumptions of modernism, its tendency toward historical discontinuity, alienation, asocial individualism, solipsism [a philosophical perspective that holds that one can only truly know oneself and that all other experiences are potentially false since they are filtered through the senses], and existentialism [a philosophy which claims that the individual must make decisions concerning right and wrong for him/herself without access to universal truths] continue to permeate contemporary writing, perhaps in a heightened sense. But the tendency of the modernist to construct intricate forms, to interweave symbols elaborately, to create works of art that, however much they oppose some established present order, create within themselves an ordered universe, have given way since the 1960s to a denial of order, to the presentation of highly fragmented universes in the created world of art, and to critical theories that are a form of phenomenology [a highly subjective contemporary philosophy which argues that the meaning of an object—a concept separate from its existence—is inherently related to the consciousness of the person perceiving it].[3]

Although the philosophies that Holman and Harmon mention are rarely the explicit subject matter of either modernist or postmodernist literature, many prominent works by authors from both periods engage in themes that relate to these philosophies indirectly. Furthermore, many of the critics responsible for the development of postmodernist theory (for example, Jacques Lacan, the members of the Frankfurt School, Michel Foucault, Roland Barthes, Jacques Derrida) have either been academically trained in philosophy themselves or substantially used the works of philosophers such as Friedrich Nietzsche, Karl Marx, Martin Heidegger, or G.W.F. Hegel as the basis for their own thought. Although the application of philosophical ideas by these critics is often radically different from that of the writers producing postmodern literature, postmodernism's inherent philosophical foundation is almost undisputed.

THE PHILOSOPHICAL BACKGROUND OF POSTMODERNISM

One of the most explicit linkages between philosophy and postmodernism came in the form of a group of Marxist social theorists who gathered at the Institute for Social Research at the University of Frankfurt in Germany beginning in 1924. This group, working in art history, linguistics, philosophy, economics, psychology, and theology, were among the first twentieth-century thinkers to interpret art within the context of all of these disciplines. In doing so, they established a radically new method of analyzing literature that moved away from aesthetics (the study of beauty) toward explanations that took social, psychological, and especially economic factors into consideration. Critic/philosophers such as Theodor W. Adorno, Georg Lukacs, Max Horkheimer, Herbert Marcuse, Walter Benjamin, and Erich Fromm became known as the first "critical theorists," a title that would be claimed in the 1960s and '70s by the critics who explicitly popularized postmodernism in its more developed stage. As David Weininger notes, the Frankfurt School's primary motivation was to find answers to the crisis of the spirit that modernist artists revealed in their work:

> While they engaged a dazzlingly diverse group of intellectual disciplines and theoretical approaches, the guiding thread of all of their analyses was the diagnosis of the ruined, pathological world of the early 20th century. Under the triumphant twin shadows of full-blown industrial capitalism and National Socialism, the Frankfurt School asked two familiar questions:

"How did we get here?" and "Where does salvation lie?" What
was so tremendously original about their collective responses
was that the answers lay not in political activism or in a revolutionary labor movement, but in such abstruse phenomena
as avant-garde art, psychoanalysis, dialectical philosophy, and
a messianic religious faith. Their studies . . . were among the
first which can be properly labeled interdisciplinary, encompassing insights from so many different areas. By the time of
their mature works—most notably Horkheimer and Adorno's
Dialectic of Enlightenment—the members of the Frankfurt
School no longer referred to their work as philosophy, sociology, aesthetics, or psychology; it was, simply, "Theory."[4]

The members of the Frankfurt School were forced into
exile by the rise to power of Adolf Hitler in 1933. Many members of the group were Jewish and their left-wing politics
were targeted by the repressive Nazi regime. They continued
their collective work in exile until the early 1940s, meeting
regularly at Columbia University in New York. Their work
would have a profound effect on a broad range of later postmodernist theorists such as Jacques Derrida, Michel Foucault, Jean Baudrillard, Linda Hutcheon, Ihab Hassan, Jürgen Habermas, and Hayden White.

Existentialism and the Early Transition to Postmodernism

World War II and the Holocaust took a tremendous toll on
the intellectual life of both Europe and, to a lesser degree,
the United States, and the unprecedented destruction of the
period deepened the sense of cynicism and pessimism that
prevailed among a sizable number of artists and philosophers. As nuclear weapons became an increasingly more
dangerous threat not only to the sovereignty of individual
countries but to the existence of life on the planet, a growing
number of intellectuals became dissatisfied with the modernist response to the twentieth-century world. For these individuals, modernism's mythic method had failed to provide
any real understanding of or relief from the pervasive mood
of gloom embodied by modernist classics like Eliot's poem
"The Waste Land" or Joyce's novel *Ulysses*. Since this mood
had only gotten worse with the deaths of millions in World
War II, the genocidal horrors of the Holocaust, and the
specter of total annihilation represented by the cold war, a
new philosophy was needed to help make sense of an increasingly senseless world.

Starting in the late 1930s and becoming increasingly popular in the 1940s and '50s, existentialist writers like Albert Camus and Jean-Paul Sartre influenced the transition from modernism to postmodernism. Both their philosophical tracts and their novels contained extensive examinations of the psychological and spiritual depression they felt was commonplace at midcentury. Works such as Sartre's *Nausea* (1938) and Camus's *The Stranger* (1942) and *The Plague* (1947) received widespread acclaim for their diagnosis of this cultural sickness, but offered few solutions other than acceptance of the relative insignificance of the individual within an indifferent universe. The major existentialist writers did not affirm that life itself was useless, but they argued that none of the institutions (e.g., religions, political parties, governments, nations, etc.) that humans had created to make order out of the world were capable of giving any enduring meaning to existence. Although Camus and Sartre were personally very active in leftist political causes, their works did not always reflect this activist mentality. In large part because of a strong reaction against its perceived nihilism (the belief that life is essentially meaningless), existentialism faded from mainstream prominence by the late 1950s and early 1960s. Its influence lingered on, though, as some of the earliest works by writers who would later be identified as prototypical postmodernists were initially identified as existentialist by many critics (for example, John Barth's novels *The Floating Opera*, published in 1956, and *The End of the Road*, published in 1958).

As existentialism waned, a second wave of critical theorists, most of whom were French, came to prominence. Foucault, Lacan, Derrida, and Barthes began formulating philosophical theories based not only on the ideas of predecessors such as the Frankfurt School, but also on an additional set of ideas taken from history, linguistics (which had become a much broader field of study that included anthropological, psychological, behavioral, and even biochemical knowledge), the physical sciences, the social sciences, and literary history. Less closely organized than the Frankfurt School, this group nevertheless produced copious quantities of work that introduced ideas and critical terms indicating a mindset that was distinctly postmodernist (i.e., after modernism) even if it still retained a number of characteristics that were borrowed or adapted from modernism. Derrida and Foucault especially were influential in creating the practice of deconstruction, a philosophical position that questions prevailing notions of truth and certainty in areas such as language, society, and even the self.

Foucault advocated a deconstructionist mode of thinking that places any "text"—which he defined as any act of expression, whether a work of literature, a spoken sentence, a textbook, or a political slogan—within a broader context that examines not just *what* is meant by it but also *how* and *why*. His theory of discourse (ordered exchange of ideas among individuals) holds that everything that can be thought, said, and felt is regulated by the world in which we live. Thus, the way the world is perceived by a particular social group at a particular time inevitably forms the rules by which that group's knowledge is produced, organized, and accepted as true. This philosophy led Foucault to reject notions of absolute truths, since the context for any statement of supposedly universal truth would always be alterable simply by changing the social or historical setting. To him, this eliminated the distinction between history and fiction, since both could and should be perceived simply as a narrative with a distinct and inevitably subjective point of view (the author's).

Expanding on ideas taken from the Swiss linguist Ferdinand de Saussure (1857–1913) and from the newly emerging field of semiotics (the study of literature and language in terms of the rules that make words have meaning), Derrida deconstructed language down to its most basic building blocks. He theorized that language is incapable of conveying the essential meaning (a so-called "signified") of anything and is instead merely a "chain of signifiers," or associations based on conventions that are understood within a given cultural context. For example, Derrida would argue that one cannot construct an indisputably true description of a bird using words. This is the case both because no collection of words is capable of fully describing a bird (only hinting at it) and because what is meant by the word *bird* changes with every situation, since the context in which the word is uttered necessarily differs in terms of time, place, cultural setting, speaker, and/or listener.

Although their methods and their terminology often differed, this first wave of genuinely postmodernist critics generally can be associated with one another on the basis of their politics (usually leftist, if not outright socialist), their skepticism about the good intentions of traditional institutions of power (governments, the academic establishment, etc.), their interest in language as a medium both for reflecting and changing culture, and their cross-disciplinary knowledge. The French theorists were not alone in their work, either. By the end of the 1960s, they were joined by North American critics like Ihab Hassan, Marshall McLuhan, and Jonathan Culler, each of whom contributed to the general understanding (and perhaps the growing confusion) surrounding the new postmodernist thinking.

YOU'RE A POSTMODERNIST AND YOU DON'T EVEN KNOW IT

At the same time that this set of critics began gaining distinction, a new group of writers—many of whom were also employed as academics—also began making a name for themselves in literature. Writers such as John Barth, Thomas Pynchon, Kurt Vonnegut Jr., Susan Sontag, Anthony Burgess, John Ashbery, and Joseph Heller began publishing works in the early 1960s that were remarkably different from the modernist style that was still the literary norm, even if its heyday had passed. Their influences included not only such modernist mainstays as Joyce and Faulkner (both of whom have, at times, been labeled with the awkward term "pre-postmodernists" to emphasize their direct influence on postmodernism) but also less traditionally acclaimed sources such as Argentinian author Jorge Luis Borges, Irish novelist Flann O'Brien, Russian émigré Vladimir Nabokov, and Irish/French playwright Samuel Beckett. As the 1960s progressed, more and more works in this vein were published and the term *postmodernist*—more commonly found in architecture at this time—began to be used to describe them, often taking the place of less satisfactory labels such as "black humor" or "fabulism."

In 1967 Barth published an essay entitled "The Literature of Exhaustion" that came to be viewed paradoxically either as a statement of purpose for postmodernist authors to follow in overturning the stale traditional order in literature or as a defense of the principles of that very same order. In this essay, he discusses his personal reasons for valuing the works of Borges, whose fantastic and complex stories were becoming ever more popular among an international audience. Barth discusses Borges's work in the context of experimental literature, making some suggestions along the way about how up-and-coming writers can help to stave off the "exhaustion" of literature by finding new ways to tell stories that have been rehashed over and over. This essay was seen by many readers as a further denunciation of the modernist reliance on mythic archetypes (e.g., Joyce's use of *The Odyssey* in writing *Ulysses*) or so-called master narratives, which were ideas that fit into the theorists' skeptical attitude toward authoritative declarations of any kind. "The Literature of Exhaustion" was cited as a refutation of established literary truths, although Barth claims his intention was more to discourage merely *imitating* modernism, rather than *emulating* it. Perhaps accidentally, Barth's essay gave validity to the idea of postmodernist literature, since one of the authors who was most frequently associated with it by critics seemed to be advocating its basic principles.

By 1979, postmodernism as a critical term was almost commonplace and works of literature that could be included within this category were dominating both the best-seller lists and the literary prize competitions. A diverse cast of writers including Barth, Donald Barthelme, Richard Brautigan, William S. Burroughs, Angela Carter, Robert Coover, LeRoi Jones, Norman Mailer, Joyce Carol Oates, Pynchon, Ishmael Reed, and Vonnegut were all affiliated (sometimes despite their own protestations) with postmodernism. Critics such as Derrida, Hassan, Foucault, and Fredric Jameson continued to elaborate their philosophical positions; Hassan's *The Dismemberment of Orpheus: Toward a Postmodernist Literature* (1971) and Jean-François Lyotard's *The Postmodern Condition: A Report on Knowledge* (1979) were especially influential studies. Furthermore, a growing number of disciples were using their ideas to study literature, not necessarily just from the contemporary period but also looking backward through literary history for works such as Laurence Sterne's *Tristram Shandy* (1767) and Miguel de Cervantes's *Don Quixote* (1615). According to Barth, such centuries-old works were now perceived as "anticipations of the 'postmodern literary aesthetic.'"[5]

Barth felt compelled to write a follow-up to "The Literature of Exhaustion" in which he again addressed postmodernism, a term that he says "was everywhere in the air"[6] in 1979. In this second essay, entitled "The Literature of Replenishment," Barth takes issue both with the lack of clarity in the application of the term *postmodernist* to literature and with the process of critical theory in general:

> One might innocently suppose that such a creature as post-
> modernism, with defined characteristics, is truly at large in
> our land. So I myself imagined when . . . I set about to learn
> what postmodernism is. . . .
>
> What I quickly discovered is that while some of the writers la-
> beled as postmodernists, myself included, may happen to take
> the label with some seriousness, a principal activity of post-
> modern critics (also called "metacritics" and "paracritics"),
> writing in postmodernist journals and speaking at postmod-
> ernist symposia, consists in disagreeing about what postmod-
> ernism is or ought to be, and thus about who should be admit-
> ted to the club—or clubbed into admission, depending upon
> the critic's view of the phenomenon and of particular writers.[7]

Barth freely admits that there are a number of writers (himself included) who write with a sensibility different from
that of Faulkner, Hemingway, or Joyce. Many of these alleged postmodernists even write detailed essays about their
innovative viewpoints on literature. Barth's complaint is that
neither *modernism* nor *postmodernism* is an especially descriptive term because of the widespread critical disagreement surrounding both. He points out that his own "novels
and stories seem to me to have both modernist and postmodernist attributes, even occasional premodernist attributes,"[8] a fact that confuses the issue even further.

THE 1980s: THE GOLDEN YEARS OF POSTMODERNISM

Despite Barth's legitimate concerns, postmodernism continued to develop in the early 1980s. As more critics contributed
more or less broad interpretations of the concept, an increasing number of authors were included under the um-
brella of postmodernism. The years of Ronald Reagan's pres-
idency (1980–1988) were a somewhat hostile environment
for leftist politics. As a result, writers such as Kathy Acker,
Toni Morrison, and Ishmael Reed, who wrote provocative
novels about race, gender, and sexuality, were often labeled
as postmodernists more for their seemingly radical literary
politics than for any particular aesthetic similarities with
such representative postmodernists as Barth or Pynchon.
Foreign writers such as Salman Rushdie, Gabriel Garcia
Marquez, Italo Calvino, and Umberto Eco gained a wide audience both in their native countries and in the United
States, acquiring reputations as postmodernists in the
process because of their stylistic originality. The predomi-

nantly South American genre of "magic realism" (typified by García Márquez's 1967 novel *One Hundred Years of Solitude*) became closely identified with postmodernism because it intentionally blurred the line between reality and imagination. Calvino's *If on a winter's night a traveler* (1979), Eco's *The Name of the Rose* (1980), and Rushdie's *Midnight's Children* (1981) were rapidly embraced by the critics as new exemplars of the postmodernist form that could stand alongside older works such as Nabokov's *Lolita* (1955), Burroughs's *Naked Lunch* (1959), Vonnegut's *Slaughterhouse-Five* (1969), or Pynchon's *Gravity's Rainbow* (1973).

Although the group of critics that had been influential in the popularization of postmodernist philosophy in the 1960s and '70s was still actively publishing, a younger generation of critics including Jean Baudrillard, Terry Eagleton, Fredric Jameson, Linda Hutcheon, Brian McHale, Gilles Deleuze, and Félix Guattari busily expanded the influence of postmodernism in literary analysis.

Especially important in this period was the French Semiotext(e) group, which published fiction by Acker and Burroughs, as well as heavily semiotics-influenced theory by Baudrillard, Deleuze and Guattari, Luce Irigaray, and other younger European critics. Whereas the older postmodernists such as Foucault and Derrida had not necessarily identified themselves with a particular political or economic position, the Semiotext(e) group was extremely anticapitalist in both their approach to writing literature and their critiques of culture. Deleuze and Guattari, for example, build on Foucault's theories about social power structures by arguing that capitalism is a schizophrenic system that in turn makes everyone in it schizophrenic. Because capitalism is interested only in the profit-making potential of the individual, the individual comes to dominate all other traditional social groupings such as the church, the family, and the working class. But at the same time, since capitalism requires social groupings in order to function, it must allow for certain controlled groupings—corporations, cartels, nations—to exist. The schizophrenia that results from this clearly affects literature, they argue, since it is the dominant philosophical context from which any literature in a capitalist environment springs. Works such as *Gravity's Rainbow* and Don DeLillo's *White Noise* (1985) are especially relevant for Deleuze and Guattari because the schizophrenia brought about by excessively materialistic capitalism is their central theme.

Baudrillard's major contributions to postmodernist theory were the related ideas of hyperreality and the simulacrum. Beginning in his 1981 work *Simulacra and Simulation*, Baudrillard argues that the prevalence of advertising, entertainment culture, and media (i.e., movies, radio, television) in contemporary life has created a situation in which simulations of life are often perceived as more real than life itself. Televised historical events such as Lee Harvey Oswald's shooting by Jack Ruby in 1963, John Hinckley's attempted assassination of Reagan in 1981, and the explosion of the space shuttle *Challenger* in 1986 are examples of this creation of hyperreality, since they presented real events in a medium that is widely perceived as a place for fictions (i.e., sitcoms, fictional dramas, miniseries, etc.). The growth of the advertising industry—a direct result of capitalism— contributes to this effect, since it intentionally distorts the reality of a product by accentuating or exaggerating its positive qualities to appeal to potential buyers. Baudrillard argues that this has created a culture in which simulated realities have as much influence on people's thinking as actual reality does. In some cases, this effect becomes so pronounced as to produce simulacra, copies of things that have no original meaning of their own. Main Street U.S.A. at Disneyland is one of Baudrillard's favorite examples of this concept—it is meant to reflect the quintessential American main street, but no real town has a main street like the one Disneyland represents. Simulacra are part of the later postmodern position that the world has become insubstantial and superficial. Novels such as Pynchon's *Vineland* (1990) and Douglas Coupland's *Generation X* (1991) also address this phenomenon without necessarily referring to Baudrillard's theories.

In the late 1980s, theorists and critics such as Charles Jencks (architecture), McHale (literature), and Jameson (philosophy) extended the reach of postmodernist thought. Simultaneously, the practitioners of postmodernist literature continued to broaden the definition of the term. The so-called brat pack writers (including Bret Easton Ellis, Tama Janowitz, and Jay McInerney) wrote novels about young adults bored with their lives in the supposedly glamorous and prosperous American cities of the 1980s. Others such as Bruce Sterling, Rudy Rucker, and William Gibson branched out into a hybrid genre incorporating postmodernist philosophies and science fiction techniques that came to be known as cyberpunk. As the 1980s drew to a close, postmodernism was both as broadly defined and as commonly used as it had ever been.

POSTMODERNISM UNDER FIRE

The early 1990s witnessed a number of events that indirectly had a negative effect on the popularity of postmodernism. The end of the cold war—often described as capitalism's victory over communism—seemed to cast doubt on the heavy anticapitalist bias of theorists like Baudrillard or Deleuze and Guattari. The Persian Gulf War in 1991 also provided Baudrillard with an opportunity to make one of his more inflammatory statements, namely that the "Gulf War Did Not Take Place" (this was the title of an essay he published less than a month after the end of the war). Baudrillard argued that the Gulf War was a media event in which the United States orchestrated a conflict in order to justify its own political power in the world through a televised demonstration of its might. This position, which is not wholly without merit, enraged enough readers to cause a sizable backlash against Baudrillard and his philosophical brothers-in-arms. As the decade progressed, postmodernist philosophy once again developed an unwanted reputation as a "fringe" movement popularized by a small but influential group of radicals on university campuses. Witness this harsh (and somewhat overstated) assessment in a 1999 article by Lynne Cheney:

> In the late 1960s and early '70s, student radicals began moving into English departments, cultivating the idea that there is no truth—and therefore no possibility of untruth. As the radicals gained power and their views spread across the university and through society, lying came to be regarded not so much as a transgression that ought to produce guilt, but as an alternative "construction," a "narrative" with all the legitimacy that the unenlightened attribute to "truth.". . .

> It was, of course, an immense leap they were making, one that was too much for most philosophy departments, where demand for a certain rigor of thought meant that "postmodernism," as this new creed came to be called, was generally held in low regard. But in departments of English, history, sociology, and art history, postmodern thought was exalted, first at elite institutions like Yale and finally almost everywhere. . . .

> By the 1980s, it was a rare student who went through college without encountering the view that there is no such thing as

truth, that the things we think are true are just the "constructs" of dominant groups. Some professors, on the grounds that there is no truth, were unabashedly using the classroom to propagate their political agendas.[9]

Cheney was not alone in accusing postmodernism of excesses. In 1996, Alan Sokal, a physics professor at New York University, published a paper entitled "Transgressing the Boundaries: Toward a Transformative Hermeneutics of Quantum Gravity" in *Social Text*, a leading journal of cultural studies. After the article was published, Sokal publicly revealed that he had submitted the article for publication as a hoax to make a point about the illogic of postmodernist rhetoric and the lack of understanding that he felt many of the most prominent postmodernist theorists showed in regard to the scientific concepts they imported into cultural studies. Sokal's admission touched off a heated debate within academic circles over the validity of his criticism and he has since become one of the most visible and most vocal detractors of postmodernism. As the millennium approached, denunciations of postmodernism's "lack of values," "unreason," or lack of appreciation for aesthetic value in art became more numerous, although both critical theorists and postmodernist writers such as the cyberpunks, DeLillo, Pynchon, Atwood, and others continued to flourish.

Despite its lack of a unified definition, postmodernism exerted a strong influence over the literature and philosophy of the last half of the twentieth century. Despite a strong faction of dissenters, aspects of its various philosophical branches remain the guiding principles for a number of younger writers and critics. Postmodernism's lack of rigidity may be its downfall or its saving grace: Either postmodernism will end up like one of Derrida's linguistic structures—just another perspective with no more essential "truth" or "meaning" than any other—or it will continue to adapt itself, as it has with cyberpunk and "X Literature" to remain relevant into the twenty-first century. Or, as some critics have argued (most likely to Barth's extreme amusement), perhaps literature is already in a postpostmodernist phase.

NOTES

1. Perry Anderson, *The Origins of Postmodernity.* London: Verso, 1998, p. 6.

2. Paula Geyh, Fred G. Leebron, and Andrew Levy, eds., *Postmodern American Fiction: A Norton Anthology.* New York: Norton, 1998, pp. xi–126.

3. C. Hugh Holman and William Harmon, eds., *A Handbook to Literature.* 6th ed. New York: Macmillan, 1992, p. 370.

4. David Weininger, "Review of *The Frankfurt School: Its History, Theories, and Political Significance* by Rolf Wiggershaus," *Boston Book Review,* March 1995, p. 11.

5. John Barth, "The Literature of Replenishment: Postmodernist Fiction" in *The Friday Book: Essays and Other Nonfiction.* New York: Putnam, 1984, p. 195.

6. Barth, "The Literature of Replenishment," p. 193.

7. Barth, "The Literature of Replenishment," p. 194.

8. Barth, "The Literature of Replenishment," p. 196.

9. Lynne Cheney, "The English Department Virus," *American Enterprise,* vol. 10, no. 3, May 1999, p. 50.

CHAPTER 1

Understanding Postmodernism

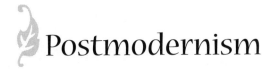 Postmodernism

The New Understanding of Language

Italo Calvino

Italo Calvino (1923–1985) was a prodigious writer, publishing dozens of books ranging from novels (see Salman Rushdie's essay on Calvino's *If on a winter's night a traveler* in this volume), short stories, literary criticism, folklore, and linguistics. His influence on the development of postmodernism is immense, both because of his technical innovations in the craft of fiction and his theoretical insights. The excerpt below is taken from a lecture he delivered in 1967 on the subject of cybernetics and language. Years before computers would revolutionize the everyday life of ordinary individuals, Calvino was already contemplating the effect that electronic media would have on human language and the literature created from it. Later critics like Jean Baudrillard and Donna Haraway brought this concept to the forefront of their models of postmodernism. Calvino discusses the ways in which perception of the nature and development of language had changed due to the work done by linguists like Noam Chomsky, and speculates about what results the interplay between science and literature might have.

It all began with the first storyteller of the tribe. Men were already exchanging articulate sounds, referring to the practical needs of their daily lives. Dialogue was already in existence, and so were the rules that it was forced to follow. This was the life of the tribe, a very complex set of rules on which every action and every situation had to be based. The number of words was limited, and, faced with the multiform world and its countless things, men defended themselves by inventing a finite number of sounds combined in various

ways. Modes of behavior, customs, and gestures too were
what they were and none other, constantly repeated while
harvesting coconuts or scavenging for wild roots, while
hunting lions or buffalo, marrying in order to create new
bonds of relationship outside the clan, or at the first moments of life, or at death. And the more limited were the
choices of phrase or behavior, the more complex the rules of
language or custom were forced to become in order to master an ever-increasing variety of situations. The extreme
poverty of ideas about the world then available to man was
matched by a detailed, all-embracing code of rules.

The storyteller began to put forth words, not because he
thought others might reply with other, predictable words,
but to test the extent to which words could fit with one another, could give birth to one another, in order to extract an
explanation of the world from the thread of every possible
spoken narrative, and from the arabesque that nouns and
verbs, subjects and predicates performed as they unfolded
from one another. The figures available to the storyteller
were very few: the jaguar, the coyote, the toucan, the pi-
ranha; or else father and son, brother-in-law and uncle, wife
and mother and sister and mother-in-law. The actions these
figures could perform were likewise rather limited: they
could be born, die, copulate, sleep, fish, hunt, climb trees,
dig burrows, eat and defecate, smoke vegetable fibers, make
prohibitions, transgress them, steal or give away fruit or
other things—things that were also classified in a limited
catalogue. The storyteller explored the possibilities implied
in his own language by combining and changing the permutations of the figures and the actions, and of the objects
on which these actions could be brought to bear. What
emerged were stories, straightforward constructions that always contained correspondences or contraries—the sky and
the earth, fire and water, animals that flew and those that
dug burrows—and each term had its array of attributes and
a repertoire of its own. The telling of stories allowed certain
relationships among the various elements and not others,
and things could happen in a certain order and not in others: prohibition had to come before transgression, punish-
ment after transgression, the gift of magic objects before the
trial of courage. The immobile world that surrounded tribal
man, strewn with signs of the fleeting correspondences between words and things, came to life in the voice of the sto-

ryteller, spun out into the flow of a spoken narrative within which each word acquired new values and transmitted them to the ideas and images they defined. Every animal, every object, every relationship took on beneficial or malign powers that came to be called magical powers but should, rather, have been called narrative powers, potentialities contained in the word, in its ability to link itself to other words on the plane of discourse.

THE STRUCTURE OF STORIES IN FOLK TALES

Primitive oral narrative, like the folk tale that has been handed down almost to the present day, is modeled on fixed structures, on, we might almost say, prefabricated elements—elements, however, that allow of an enormous number of combinations. Vladimir Propp, in the course of his studies of Russian folk tales, came to the conclusion that all such tales were like variants of a single tale, and could be broken down into a limited number of narrative functions. Forty years later Claude Lévi-Strauss, working on the myths of the Indians of Brazil, saw these as a system of logical operations between permutable terms, so that they could be studied according to the mathematical processes of combinatorial analysis.

Even if the folk imagination is therefore not boundless like the ocean, there is no reason to think of it as being like a water tank of small capacity. On an equal level of civilization, the operations of narrative, like those of mathematics, cannot differ all that much from one people to another, but what can be constructed on the basis of these elementary processes can present unlimited combinations, permutations, and transformations.

NARRATIVE STRUCTURES

Is this true only of oral narrative traditions? Or can it be maintained of literature in all its variety of forms and complexities? As early as the 1920s, the Russian Formalists began to make modern stories and novels the object of their analysis, breaking down their complex structures into functional segments. In France today the semiological school of Roland Barthes, having sharpened its knives on the structures of advertising or of women's fashion magazines, is at last turning its attention to literature; the eighth issue of the magazine *Communications* was devoted to the structural analysis of the short story. Naturally enough, the material that lends itself best to this kind of treatment is still to be found in the various forms of popular fiction. If the Russians studied the Sherlock Holmes stories, today it is James Bond who provides the structuralists with their most apt exemplars.

But this is merely the first step in the grammar and syntax of narrative fiction. The combinatorial play of narrative possibilities soon passes beyond the level of content to touch upon the relationship of the narrator to the material related and to the reader: and this brings us to the toughest set of problems facing contemporary fiction. It is no coincidence that the researches of the French structuralists go hand in hand (and sometimes coexist in the same person) with the creative work of the "Tel Quel" group. For the latter—and here I am paraphrasing statements by one of their authorized interpreters—writing consists no longer in narrating but in saying that one is narrating, and what one says becomes identified with the very act of saying. The psychological person is replaced by a linguistic or even a grammatical person, defined solely by his place in the discourse. These formal repercussions of a literature at the second or third degree, such as occurred in France with the *nouveau roman* of [the 1950s], for which another of its exponents suggested the word "scripturalism," can be traced back to combinations of a certain number of logico-linguistic (or better, syntactical-rhetorical) operations, in such a way as to be reducible to formulas that are the more general as they become less complex.

The Influence of New Knowledge on Language

I will not go into technical details on which I could only be an unauthorized and rather unreliable commentator. My intention here is merely to sum up the situation, to make connections between a number of books I have recently read, and to put these in the context of a few general reflections. In the particular way today's culture looks at the world, one tendency is emerging from several directions at once. The world in its various aspects is increasingly looked upon as *discrete* rather than *continuous*. I am using the term "discrete" in the sense it bears in mathematics, a discrete quantity being one made up of separate parts. Thought, which until the other day appeared to us as something fluid, evoking linear images such as a flowing river or an unwinding thread, or else gaseous images such as a kind of vaporous cloud—to the point where it was sometimes called "spirit"

(in the sense of "breath")—we now tend to think of as a series of discontinuous states, of combinations of impulses acting on a finite (though enormous) number of sensory and
motor organs. Electronic brains, even if they are still far
from producing all the functions of the human brain, are
nonetheless capable of providing us with a convincing theoretical model for the most complex processes of our memory, our mental associations, our imagination, our conscience. Shannon, Weiner, von Neumann, and Turing have
radically altered our image of our mental processes. In the
place of the ever-changing cloud that we carried in our
heads until the other day, the condensing and dispersal of
which we attempted to understand by describing impalpable
psychological states and shadowy landscapes of the soul—in
the place of all this we now feel the rapid passage of signals
on the intricate circuits that connect the relays, the diodes,
the transistors with which our skulls are crammed. Just as
no chess player will ever live long enough to exhaust all the
combinations of possible moves for the thirty-two pieces on
the chessboard, so we know (given the fact that our minds
are chessboards with hundreds of billions of pieces) that not
even in a lifetime lasting as long as the universe would one
ever manage to make all possible plays. But we also know
that all these are implicit in the overall code of mental plays,
according to the rules by which each of us, from one moment to the next, formulates his thoughts, swift or sluggish,
cloudy or crystalline as they may be.

I might also say that what is finite and numerically calcu-
lable is superseding the indeterminateness of ideas that
cannot be subjected to measurement and delimitation; but
this formulation runs the risk of giving an oversimplified
notion of how things stand. In fact, the very opposite is true:
every analytical process, every division into parts, tends to
provide an image of the world that is ever more complicated,
just as Zeno of Elea, by refusing to accept space as continuous, ended up by separating Achilles from the tortoise by an
infinite number of intermediate points. But mathematical
complexity can be digested instantly by electronic brains.
Their abacus of only two numerals permits them to make
instantaneous calculations of a complexity unthinkable for
human brains. They have only to count on two fingers to
bring into play incredibly rapid matrices of astronomical
sums. One of the most arduous intellectual efforts of the

Middle Ages has only now become entirely real: I refer to the Catalan monk Raymond Lully and his *ars combinatoria.*

The process going on today is the triumph of discontinuity, divisibility, and combination over all that is flux, or a series of minute nuances following one upon the other. The nineteenth century, from Hegel to Darwin, saw the triumph of historical continuity and biological continuity as they healed all the fractures of dialectical antitheses and genetic mutations. Today this perspective is radically altered. In history we no longer follow the course of a spirit immanent in the events of the world, but the curves of statistical diagrams, and historical research is leaning more and more toward mathematics. And as for biology, Watson and Crick have shown us how the transmission of the characteristics of the species consists in the duplication of a certain number of spiral-shaped molecules formed from a certain number of acids and bases. In other words, the endless variety of living forms can be reduced to the combination of certain finite quantities. Here again, it is information theory that imposes its patterns. The processes that appeared most resistant to a formulation in terms of number, to a quantitative description, are not translated into mathematical patterns.

Born and raised on quite different terrain, structural linguistics tends to appear in terms of a play of contraries every bit as simple as information theory. And linguists, too, have begun to talk in terms of codes and messages, to attempt to establish the entropy of language on all levels, including that of literature.

LINGUISTICS AND LITERATURE COME TOGETHER

Mankind is beginning to understand how to dismantle and reassemble the most complex and unpredictable of all its machines: language. Today's world is far richer in words and concepts and signs than the world that surrounded primitive man, and the uses of the various levels of language are a great deal more complex. Using transformational mathematical patterns, the American school led by [Noam] Chomsky is exploring the deep structure of language, lying at the roots of the logical processes that may constitute no longer a historical characteristic of man, but a biological one. And extreme simplification of logical formulas, on the other hand, is used by the French school of structural semantics headed by A.J. Greimas. This school analyzes the narrative quality of all discourse, which may be reduced to a ratio between what they call *actants*.

After a gap of almost thirty years, a "Neo-Formalist" school has been reborn in the Soviet Union, employing the results of cybernetic research and structural semiology for the analysis of literature. Headed by a mathematician, Kholmogorov, this school carries out studies of a highly academic scientific nature based on the calculation of probabilities and the quantity of information contained in poems.

A further encounter between mathematics and literature is taking place in France, under the banner of hoaxing and practical joking. This is the Ouvroir de Littérature Potentielle (Oulipo), founded by Raymond Queneau and a number of his mathematician friends. This almost clandestine group of ten people is an offshoot of the Collège de Pataphysique, the literary society founded in memory of Alfred Jarry as a kind of academy of intellectual scorn. Meanwhile, the researches of Oulipo into the mathematical structure of the sestina in the work of the Provençal troubadours and of Dante are no less austere than the studies of the Soviet cyberneticists. It should not be forgotten that Queneau is the author of a book called *Cent Mille Milliards de poèmes [A Hundred Thousand Billion Poems]*, which purports to be not so much a book as the rudimentary model of a machine for making sonnets, each one different from the last.

LITERATURE FROM A MACHINE

Having laid down these procedures and entrusted a computer with the task of carrying out these operations, will we have a machine capable of replacing the poet and the author? Just as we already have machines that can read, machines that perform a linguistic analysis of literary texts, machines that make translations and summaries, will we also have machines capable of conceiving and composing poems and novels?

The interesting thing is not so much the question whether this problem is soluble in practice—because in any case it would not be worth the trouble of constructing such a complicated machine—as the theoretical possibility of it, which would give rise to a series of unusual conjectures. And I am not now thinking of a machine capable merely of "assembly-line" literary production, which would already be mechanical in itself. I am thinking of a writing machine that would bring to the page all those things that we are accustomed to consider as the most jealously guarded attributes of our psychological life, of our daily experience, our unpredictable changes of mood and inner elations, despairs and moments of illumination. What are these if not so many linguistic "fields," for which we might well succeed in establishing the vocabulary, grammar, syntax, and properties of permutation?

What would be the style of a literary automaton? I believe that its true vocation would be for classicism. The test of a poetic-electronic machine would be its ability to produce traditional works, poems with closed metrical forms, novels that follow all the rules. In this sense the use so far made of machines by the literary avant-garde is still too human. Especially in Italy, the machine used in these experiments is an instrument of chance, of the destructuralization of form, of protest against every habitual logical connection. I would therefore say that it is still an entirely lyrical instrument, serving a typical human need: the production of disorder. The true literature machine will be one that itself feels the need to produce disorder, as a reaction against its preceding production of order: a machine that will produce avant-garde work to free its circuits when they are choked by too long a production of classicism. In fact, given that developments in cybernetics lean toward machines capable of learning, of changing their own programs, of developing their own sensibilities and their own needs, nothing prevents us from foreseeing a literature machine that at a certain point feels unsatisfied with its own traditionalism and starts to propose new ways of writing, turning its own codes completely upside down. To gratify critics who look for similarities between things literary and things historical, sociological, or economic, the machine could correlate its own changes of style to the variations in certain statistical indices of production, or income, or military expenditure, or the distribution of decision-making powers. That indeed will be the literature that corresponds perfectly to a theoretical hypothesis: it will, at last, be *the* literature.

Ten Points About Postmodernism

Ihab Hassan

Ihab Hassan, professor of English and comparative literature at the University of Wisconsin at Milwaukee, is often referred to as the "father of postmodernism" in light of his more than four decades of critical examination of innovations in contemporary literature. This selection is taken from his 1987 article "Toward a Concept of Postmodernism," which proved to be extremely significant in the development of the understanding of postmodernism in the 1990s and beyond. Without necessarily wanting to claim philosophical or aesthetic superiority for postmodernism, Hassan acknowledges that the works of a substantial group of thinkers and artists have something in common with each other that can be called postmodernism. Hassan first provides a useful list of figures from various disciplines that fall under a broad definition of postmodernism and then poses a set of ten questions that he feels must be addressed before postmodernism can be fully integrated into the vocabulary of literary criticism. Hassan's vocabulary, as should be expected, is extensive, but (unlike many other postmodern critics) he writes without using a great deal of specialized critical jargon.

The strains of silence in literature, from [the Marquis de] Sade to [Samuel] Beckett, convey complexities of language, culture, and consciousness as these contest themselves and one another. Such eerie music may yield an experience, an intuition, of postmodernism but no concept or definition of it. Perhaps I can move here toward such a concept by putting forth certain queries. I begin with the most obvious: can we really perceive a phenomenon, in Western societies generally and in their literatures particularly, that needs to be distinguished from modernism, needs to be named? If so, will the provisional rubric "postmodernism" serve? Can we then—or even should we at this time—construct of this phenomenon some probative scheme, both chronological and typological, that may account for its various trends and counter-trends, its artistic, epistemic, and social character? And how would this phenomenon—let us call it postmodernism—relate itself to such earlier modes of change as turn-of-the-century avantgardes or the high modernism of the twenties? Finally, what difficulties would inhere in any such act of definition? . . .

Some names, piled here pell-mell, may serve to adumbrate postmodernism, or at least suggest its range of assumptions: Jacques Derrida, Jean-François Lyotard (philosophy), Michel Foucault, Hayden White (history), Jacques Lacan, Gilles Deleuze, R.D. Laing, Norman O. Brown (psychoanalysis), Herbert Marcuse, Jean Baudrillard, Jürgen Habermas (political philosophy), Thomas Kuhn, Paul Feyerabend (philosophy of science), Roland Barthes, Julia Kristeva, Wolfgang Iser, the "Yale Critics" (literary theory), Merce Cunningham, Alwin Nikolais, Meredith Monk (dance), John Cage, Karlheinz Stockhausen, Pierre Boulez (music), Robert Rauschenberg, Jean Tinguely, Joseph Beuys (art), Robert Venturi, Charles Jencks, Brent Bolin (architecture), and various authors from Samuel Beckett, Eugène Ionesco, Jorge Luis Borges, Max Bense, and Vladimir Nabokov to Harold Pinter, B.S. Johnson, Rayner Heppenstall, Christine Brooke-Rose, Helmut Heissenbüttel, Jürgen Becker, Peter Handke, Thomas Bernhardt, Ernst Jandl, Gabriel García Márquez, Julio Cortázar, Alain Robbe-Grillet, Michel Butor, Maurice Roche, Philippe Sollers, and, in America, John Barth, William Burroughs, Thomas Pynchon, Donald Barthelme, Walter Abish, John Ashbery, David Antin, Sam Shepard, and Robert Wilson. Indubitably, these names are far too heterogenous to form a movement, paradigm, or school. Still, they may evoke a number of related cultural tendencies, a constellation of values, a repertoire of procedures and attitudes. These we call *postmodernism.* . . .

THE POSTMODERN ERA

I do not mean to take my stand with the postmoderns against the (ancient) moderns. In an age of frantic intellectual fashions, values can be too recklessly voided, and tomorrow can quickly preempt today or yesteryear. Nor is it merely a matter of fashions; for the sense of supervention may express some cultural urgency that partakes less of hope than fear. This much we recall: Lionel Trilling entitled one of his most thoughtful works *Beyond Culture* (1965); Kenneth Boulding argued that "postcivilization" is an essential part of *The Meaning of the 20th Century* (1964); and George Steiner could have subtitled his essay, *In Bluebeard's Castle* (1971), "Notes Toward the Definition of Postculture." Before them, Roderick Seidenberg published his *Post-Historic Man* exactly in mid-century; and most recently, I have myself speculated, in *The Right Promethean Fire* (1980), about the advent of a posthumanist era. As Daniel Bell put it: "It used to be that the great literary modifier was the word *beyond*. . . . But we seem to have exhausted the beyond, and today the sociological modifier is *post*."

My point here is double: in the question of postmodernism, there is a will and counter-will to intellectual power, an imperial desire of the mind, but this will and desire are themselves caught in a historical moment of supervention, if not exactly of obsolescence. The reception or denial of postmodernism thus remains contingent on the psychopolitics of academic life—including the various dispositions of people and power in our universities, of critical factions and personal frictions, of boundaries that arbitrarily include or exclude—no less than on the imperatives of the culture at large. This much, reflexivity seems to demand from us at the start.

But reflection demands also that we address a number of conceptual problems that both conceal and constitute postmodernism itself. I shall try to isolate ten of these, commencing with the simpler, moving toward the more intractable.

Questions Raised by Postmodernism

1. The word postmodernism sounds not only awkward, uncouth; it evokes what it wishes to surpass or suppress, modernism itself. The term thus contains its enemy within, as the terms romanticism and classicism, baroque and rococo, do not. Moreover, it denotes temporal linearity and connotes belatedness, even decadence, to which no postmodernist would admit. But what better name have we to give this curious age? The Atomic, or Space, or Television, Age? These technological tags lack theoretical definition. Or shall we

call it the Age of Indetermanence (indeterminacy + immanence) as I have half-antically proposed? Or better still, shall we simply live and let others live to call us what they may?

2. Like other categorical terms—say poststructuralism, or modernism, or romanticism for that matter—postmodernism suffers from a certain *semantic* instability: that is, no clear consensus about its meaning exists among scholars. The general difficulty is compounded in this case by two factors: (a) the relative youth, indeed brash adolescence, of the term postmodernism, and (b) its semantic kinship to more current terms, themselves equally unstable. Thus some critics mean by postmodernism what others call avant-gardism or even neo-avant-gardism, while still others would call the same phenomenon simply modernism. This can make for inspired debates.

3. A related difficulty concerns the *historical* instability of many literary concepts, their openness to change. Who, in this epoch of fierce misprisions, would dare to claim that romanticism is apprehended by [poet Samuel Taylor] Coleridge, [essayist Walter] Pater, [historian A.O.] Lovejoy, [critic M.H.] Abrams, [critic Morse] Peckham, and [critic Harold] Bloom in quite the same way? There is already some evidence that postmodernism, and modernism even more, are beginning to slip and slide in time, threatening to make any diacritical distinction between them desperate. But perhaps the phenomenon, akin to Hubble's "red shift" in astronomy, may someday serve to measure the historical velocity of literary concepts.

4. Modernism and postmodernism are not separated by an Iron Curtain or Chinese Wall; for history is a palimpsest, and culture is permeable to time past, time present, and time future. We are all, I suspect, a little Victorian, Modern, and Postmodern, at once. And an author may, in his or her own life time, easily write both a modernist and postmodernist work. (Contrast [James] Joyce's *Portrait of the Artist as a Young Man* with his *Finnegans Wake.*) More generally, on a certain level of narrative abstraction, modernism itself may be rightly assimilated to romanticism, romanticism related to the enlightenment, the latter to the renaissance, and so back, if not to the Olduvai Gorge [i.e. human origins], then certainly to ancient Greece.

5. This means that a "period," as I have already intimated, must be perceived in terms *both* of continuity *and* disconti-

nuity, the two perspectives being complementary and partial. The Apollonian view, rangy and abstract, discerns only
historical conjunctions; the Dionysian feeling, sensuous
though nearly purblind, touches only the disjunctive moment. Thus postmodernism, by invoking two divinities at
once, engages a double view. Sameness and difference, unity
and rupture, filiation and revolt, all must be honored if we
are to attend to history, apprehend (perceive, understand)
change both as a spatial, mental structure and as a temporal, physical process, both as pattern and unique event.

6. Thus a "period" is generally not a period at all; it is
rather both a diachronic and synchronic construct. Postmodernism, again like modernism or romanticism, is no ex-
ception; it requires *both* historical *and* theoretical definition.
We would not seriously claim an inaugural "date" for it as
Virginia Woolf pertly did for modernism, though we may
sometimes woefully imagine that postmodernism began "in
or about September, 1939." Thus we continually discover
"antecedents" of postmodernism. . . . What this really indi-
cates is that we have created in our mind a model of postmodernism, a particular typology of culture and imagination, and have proceeded to "rediscover" the affinities of
various authors and different moments with that model. We
have, that is, reinvented our ancestors—and always shall.
Consequently, "older" authors can be postmodern—[Franz]
Kafka, [Samuel] Beckett, [Jorge-Luis] Borges, [Vladimir]
Nabokov, [Witold] Gombrowicz—while "younger" authors
need not be so—[William] Styron, [John] Updike, [Truman]
Capote, [John] Irving, [E.L.] Doctorow, [John] Gardner.

7. As we have seen, any definition of postmodernism calls
upon a fourfold vision of complementarities, embracing continuity and discontinuity, diachrony and synchrony. But a definition of the concept also requires a dialectical vision; for
defining traits are often antithetical, and to ignore this tendency of historical reality is to lapse into single vision and
Newton's sleep. Defining traits are dialectical and also plural;
to elect a single trait as an absolute criterion of postmodern
grace is to make of all other writers preterites. Thus we can
not simply rest—as I have sometimes done—on the assump-
tion that postmodernism is antiformal, anarchic, or decre-
ative; for though it is indeed all these, and despite its fanatic
will to unmaking, it also contains the need to discover [as Susan Sontag notes] a "unitary sensibility," to "cross the border

and close the gap" [as Leslie Fiedler states], and to attain, as I have suggested, an immanence of discourse, an expanded noetic intervention, a "neo-gnostic im-mediacy of mind."

8. All this leads to the prior problem of periodization itself, which is also that of literary history conceived as a particular apprehension of change. Indeed, the concept of postmodernism implies some theory of innovation, renovation, novation, or simply change. But which one? Heraclitean? Viconian? Darwinian? Marxist? Freudian? Kuhnian? Derridean? Eclectic? Or is a "theory of change" itself an oxymoron best suited to ideologues intolerant of the ambiguities of time? Should postmodernism, then, be left—at least for the moment—unconceptualized, a kind of literary-historical "difference" or "trace"?

9. Postmodernism can expand into a still larger problem: is it only an artistic tendency or also a social phenomenon, perhaps even a mutation in Western humanism? If so, how are the various aspects of this phenomenon—psychological, philosophical, economic, political—joined or disjoined? In short, can we understand postmodernism in literature without some attempt to perceive the lineaments of a postmodern society, a Toynbeean [i.e. derived from the ideas of historian Arnold Toynbee] postmodernity, or future Foucauldian [derived from the theories of philosopher Michel Foucault] *épistémè*, of which the literary tendency I have been discussing is but a single, elitist strain?

10. Finally, though not least vexing, is postmodernism an honorific term, used insidiously to valorize writers, however disparate, whom we otherwise esteem, to hail trends, however discordant, which we somehow approve? Or is it, on the contrary, a term of opprobrium and objurgation? In short, is postmodernism a descriptive as well as evaluative or normative category of literary thought? Or does it belong, as Charles Altieri notes, to that category of "essentially contested concepts" in philosophy that never wholly exhaust their constitutive confusions?

No doubt, other conceptual problems lurk in the matter of postmodernism. Such problems, however, can not finally inhibit the intellectual imagination, the desire to apprehend our historical presence in noetic constructs that reveal our being to ourselves. I move, therefore, to propose a provisional scheme that the literature of silence, from Sade to Beckett, seems to envisage, and do so by distinguishing, tentatively, between three modes of artistic change in the last hundred years. I call these avant-garde, modern, and post-modern, though I realize that all three have conspired to-gether to create that "tradition of the new" that, since [Charles] Baudelaire, brought "into being an art whose his-tory regardless of the credos of its practitioners, has con-sisted of leaps from vanguard to vanguard, and political mass movements whose aim has been the total renovation not only of social institutions but of man himself."

Irony as the Defining Principle of Postmodernism

Umberto Eco

Umberto Eco, professor of semiotics at the University
of Bologna in Italy, is also the author of one of the
central works of postmodern fiction. His 1980 novel
The Name of the Rose, set in an Italian monastery in
the fourteenth century, is a mainstay of "must-read"
lists of postmodernism. *Foucault's Pendulum* (1989),
his second novel, contains an elaborate plot that
works both as a mystery novel and as a treatise on
the process of writing a postmodern book. As a
scholar of both linguistics and literature, Eco is a
skilled critic as well as a successful novelist. The excerpt below is taken from his supplementary volume
to *The Name of the Rose*. Eco discusses some of the
techniques he used in creating his fictional master-
piece as well as addressing some of the critical reaction to it. In this selection, Eco discusses the prominent role that irony plays in separating modernism
from postmodernism, even though he has some
reservations about the latter term. Instead of being a
negative force as it was in modernist literature, Eco
argues that postmodern irony actually revitalizes art
that has in some way reached its limits of expression. This revitalized literature in turn stimulates
new potential for enjoyment in its readers.

Between 1965 and today [1983], two ideas have been defini-
tively clarified: that plot could be found also in the form of
quotation of other plots, and that the quotation could be less
escapist than the plot quoted. . . . The real problem at stake
then was, could there be a novel that was not escapist and,
nevertheless, still enjoyable?

Excerpted from "Postmodernism, Irony, the Enjoyable," in *Postscript to "The Name of the Rose."* Copyright © 1983 by Umberto Eco. English translation copyright © 1984 by Harcourt, Inc. Reprinted by permission of the publisher.

This link, and the rediscovery not only of plot but also of enjoyability, was to be realized by the American theorists of postmodernism.

Unfortunately, "postmodern" is a term *bon à tout faire* ["good to use everywhere"]. I have the impression that it is applied today to anything the user of the term happens to like. Further, there seems to be an attempt to make it increasingly retroactive: first it was apparently applied to certain writers or artists active in the last twenty years, then gradually it reached the beginning of the century, then still further back. And this reverse procedure continues; soon the postmodern category will include Homer.

Actually, I believe that postmodernism is not a trend to be chronologically defined, but, rather, an ideal category—or, better still, a *Kunstwollen* [literally, "an artistic want"], a way of operating. We could say that every period has its own postmodernism, just as every period would have its own mannerism (and, in fact, I wonder if postmodernism is not the modern name for mannerism as metahistorical category). I believe that in every period there are moments of crisis like those described by [philosopher Friedrich] Nietzsche in his *Thoughts Out of Season*, in which he wrote about the harm done by historical studies. The past conditions us, harries us, blackmails us. The historic avant-garde (but here I would also consider avant-garde a metahistorical category) tries to settle scores with the past. . . . The avant-garde destroys, defaces the past. . . . Then the avant-garde goes further, destroys the figure, cancels it, arrives at the abstract, the informal, the white canvas, the slashed canvas, the charred canvas. In architecture and the visual arts, it will be the curtain wall, the building as stele, pure parallelepiped, minimal art; in literature, the destruction of the flow of discourse, the [William] Burroughs-like collage, silence, the white page; in music, the passage from atonality to noise to absolute silence (in this sense, the early [composer John] Cage is modern).

WHEN MODERNISM BECOMES POSTMODERNISM

But the moment comes when the avant-garde (the modern) can go no further, because it has produced a metalanguage that speaks of its impossible texts (conceptual art). The postmodern reply to the modern consists of recognizing that the past, since it cannot really be destroyed, because its destruc-

A LITERARY SHOPPING LIST

Don DeLillo's White Noise *is generally considered a prime example of postmodern fiction. This excerpt from the novel consists of the first two paragraphs of the novel, in which DeLillo begins to record the avalanche of consumer goods that he claims have come to define American culture. In this way,* White Noise *demonstrates Eco's claims about the importance of irony in postmodern literature, since DeLillo makes literature out of the distinctly unliterary language of advertising.*

The station wagons arrived at noon, a long shining line that coursed through the west campus. In single file they eased around the orange I-beam sculpture and moved toward the dormitories. The roofs of the station wagons were loaded down with carefully secured suitcases full of light and heavy clothing; with boxes of blankets, boots and shoes, stationery and books, sheets, pillows, quilts; with rolled-up rugs and sleeping bags; with bicycles, skis, rucksacks, English and Western saddles, inflated rafts. As cars slowed to a crawl and stopped, students sprang out and raced to the rear doors to begin removing the objects inside; the stereo sets, radios, personal computers; small refrigerators and table ranges; the cartons of phonograph records and cassettes; the hairdryers and styling irons; the tennis rackets, soccer balls, hockey and lacrosse sticks, bows and arrows; the controlled substances, the birth control pills and devices; the junk food still in shopping bags—onion-and-garlic chips, nacho thins, peanut creme patties, Waffelos and Kabooms, fruit chews and toffee popcorn; the Dum-Dum pops, the Mystic mints.

I've witnessed this spectacle every September for twenty-one years. It is a brilliant event, invariably. The students greet each other with comic cries and gestures of sodden collapse. Their summer has been bloated with criminal pleasures, as always. The parents stand sun-dazed near their automobiles, seeing images of themselves in every direction. The conscientious suntans. The well-made faces and wry looks. They feel a sense of renewal, of communal recognition. The women crisp and alert, in diet trim, knowing people's names. Their husbands content to measure out the time, distant but ungrudging, accomplished in parenthood, something about them suggesting massive insurance coverage. This assembly of station wagons, as much as anything they might do in the course of the year, more than formal liturgies or laws, tells the parents they are a collection of the like-minded and the spiritually akin, a people, a nation.

Don DeLillo, *White Noise.* New York: Penguin, 1986, pp. 3–4.

tion leads to silence, must be revisited: but with irony, not innocently. I think of the postmodern attitude as that of a man who loves a very cultivated woman and knows he cannot say to her, "I love you madly," because he knows that she knows (and that she knows that he knows) that these words have already been written by Barbara Cartland. Still, there is a solution. He can say, "As Barbara Cartland would put it, I love you madly." At this point, having avoided false innocence, having said clearly that it is no longer possible to speak innocently, he will nevertheless have said what he wanted to say to the woman: that he loves her, but he loves her in an age of lost innocence. If the woman goes along with this, she will have received a declaration of love all the same. Neither of the two speakers will feel innocent, both will have accepted the challenge of the past, of the already said, which cannot be eliminated; both will consciously and with pleasure play the game of irony. . . . But both will have succeeded, once again, in speaking of love.

Irony, metalinguistic play, enunciation squared. Thus, with the modern, anyone who does not understand the game can only reject it, but with the postmodern, it is possible not to understand the game and yet to take it seriously. Which is, after all, the quality (the risk) of irony. There is always someone who takes ironic discourse seriously. I think that the collages of Picasso, Juan Gris, and Braque were modern: this is why normal people would not accept them. On the other hand, the collages of Max Ernst, who pasted together bits of nineteenth-century engravings, were postmodern: they can be read as fantastic stories, as the telling of dreams, without any awareness that they amount to a discussion of the nature of engraving, and perhaps even of collage. If "postmodern" means this, it is clear why [eighteenth-century author Lawrence] Sterne and [Renaissance author François] Rabelais were postmodern, why [twentieth-century author Jorge Luis] Borges surely is, and why in the same artist the modern moment and the postmodern moment can coexist, or alternate, or follow each other closely. Look at [James] Joyce. The *Portrait* [*of an Artist as a Young Man*] is the story of an attempt at the modern. *Dubliners*, even if it comes before, is more modern than *Portrait*. *Ulysses* is on the borderline. *Finnegans Wake* is already postmodern, or at least it initiates the postmodern discourse: it demands, in order to be understood, not the negation of the already said, but its ironic rethinking.

THE CONTINUING DEBATE OVER POSTMODERNISM

On the subject of the postmodern nearly everything has been said, from the very beginning (namely, in essays like "The Literature of Exhaustion" by John Barth, which dates from 1967). Not that I am entirely in agreement with the grades that the theoreticians of postmodernism (Barth included) give to writers and artists, establishing who is postmodern and who has not yet made it. But I am interested in the theorem that the trend's theoreticians derive from their premises: "My ideal postmodernist author neither merely repudiates nor merely imitates either his twentieth-century modernist parents or his nineteenth-century premodernist grandparents. He has the first half of our century under his belt, but not on his back. . . . He may not hope to reach and move the devotees of James Michener and Irving Wallace—not to mention the lobotomized mass-media illiterates. But he *should* hope to reach and delight, at least part of the time, beyond the circle of what [Thomas] Mann used to call the Early Christians: professional devotees of high art. . . . The ideal postmodernist novel will somehow rise above the quarrel between realism and irrealism, formalism and "contentism," pure and committed literature, coterie fiction and junk fiction. . . . My own analogy would be with good jazz or classical music: one finds much on successive listenings or close examination of the score that one didn't catch the first time through; but the first time through should be so ravishing— and not just to specialists—that one delights in the replay."

This is what Barth wrote in 1980, resuming the discussion, but this time under the title "The Literature of Replenishment: Postmodernist Fiction." Naturally, the subject can be discussed further, with a greater taste for paradox; and this is what Leslie Fiedler does. In 1980 *Salmagundi* (no. 50–51) published a debate between Fiedler and other American authors. Fiedler, obviously, is out to provoke. He praises *The Last of the Mohicans*, adventure stories, Gothic novels, junk scorned by critics that was nevertheless able to create myths and capture the imagination of more than one generation. He wonders if something like *Uncle Tom's Cabin* will ever appear again, a book that can be read with equal passion in the kitchen, the living room, and the nursery. He includes Shakespeare among those who knew how to amuse, along with *Gone with the Wind.* We all know he is too keen a critic to believe these things. He simply wants to break down the barrier that has been erected between art and enjoyability. He feels that today reaching a vast public and capturing its dreams perhaps means acting as the avant-garde, and he still leaves us free to say that capturing readers' dreams does not necessarily mean encouraging escape: it can also mean haunting them.

Postmodernism and the Art of Writing

Donald Barthelme

Before his death in 1989, Donald Barthelme was one of the most prodigious authors of postmodern fiction. He published four novels—*Snow White* being the most renowned—and several collections of short stories. Additionally, he contributed a considerable number of essays and critical articles to popular and scholarly publications in which he often discussed his idiosyncratic views on the nature of art and literature. In the excerpt that follows, Barthelme describes his views on the role of a writer by demonstrating the process of creating a story. He argues that the process of writing is a sorting out of things that are not and cannot be known until they are written. The "story" that he constructs in the course of the essay is as much a demonstration of the postmodern author in action as it is a comment on the difficulties that a writer faces in the postmodern era.

Let us suppose that someone is writing a story. From the world of conventional signs he takes an azalea bush, plants it in a pleasant park. He takes a gold pocket watch from the world of conventional signs and places it under the azalea bush. He takes from the same rich source a handsome thief and a chastity belt, places the thief in the chastity belt and lays him tenderly under the azalea, not neglecting to wind the gold pocket watch so that its ticking will, at length, awaken the now-sleeping thief. From the Sarah Lawrence campus he borrows a pair of seniors, Jacqueline and Jemima, and sets them to walking in the vicinity of the azalea bush and the handsome, chaste thief. Jacqueline and Jemima have just failed the Graduate Record Examination and are cursing God in colorful Sarah Lawrence language.

What happens next?

Of course, I don't know.

It's appropriate to pause and say that the writer is one who, embarking upon a task, does not know what to do. I cannot tell you, at this moment, whether Jacqueline and Jemima will succeed or fail in their effort to jimmy the chastity belt's lock, or whether the thief, whose name is Zeno and who has stolen the answer sheets for the next set of Graduate Record Examinations, will pocket the pocket watch or turn it over to the nearest park employee. The fate of the azalea bush, whether it will bloom or strangle in a killing frost, is unknown to me.

A very conscientious writer might purchase an azalea at the Downtown Nursery and a gold watch at Tiffany's, hire a handsome thief fresh from Riker's island, obtain the loan of a chastity belt from the Metropolitan, inveigle Jacqueline and Jemima in from Bronxville, and arrange them all under glass for study, writing up the results in honest, even fastidious prose. But in so doing he places himself in the realm of journalism or sociology. The not-knowing is crucial to art, is what permits art to be made. Without the scanning process engendered by not-knowing, without the possibility of having the mind move in unanticipated directions, there would be no invention.

This is not to say that I don't know anything about Jacqueline or Jemima, but what I do know comes into being at the instant it's inscribed. Jacqueline, for example, loathes her mother, whereas Jemima dotes on hers—I discover this by writing the sentence that announces it. Zeno was fathered by a—what? Polar bear? Roller skate? Shower of gold? I opt for the shower of gold, for Zeno is a hero (although he's just become one by virtue of his golden parent). Inside the pocket watch there is engraved a legend. Can I make it out? I think so: *Drink me*, it says. No no, can't use it, that's Lewis Carroll's. But could Zeno be a watch swallower rather than a thief? No again, Zeno'd choke on it, and so would the reader. There are rules.

Writing is a process of dealing with not-knowing, a forcing of what and how. We have all heard novelists testify to the fact that, beginning a new book, they are utterly baffled as to how to proceed, what should be written and how it might be written, even though they've done a dozen. At best there's a slender intuition, not much greater than an itch. The anxiety attached to this situation is not inconsiderable.

"Nothing to paint and nothing to paint with," as [Samuel] Beckett says of Bram van Velde. The not-knowing is not simple, because it's hedged about with prohibitions, roads that may not be taken. The more serious the artist, the more problems he takes into account and the more considerations limit his possible initiatives—a point to which I shall return.

What kind of a fellow is Zeno? How do I know until he's opened his mouth?

"Gently, ladies, gently," says Zeno, as Jacqueline and Jemima bash away at the belt with a spade borrowed from a friendly park employee. And to the park employee: "Somebody seems to have lost this-here watch."

Let us change the scene.

Alphonse, the park employee from the preceding episode, he who lent the spade, is alone in his dismal room on West Street (I could position him as well in a four-story townhouse on East Seventy-second, but you'd object, and rightly so; verisimilitude forbids it, nothing's calculated quicker than a salary). Alphonse, like so many toilers in the great city, is not as simple as he seems. Like those waiters who are really actors and those cab drivers who are really composers of electronic music, Alphonse is sunlighting as a Parks Department employee although he is, in reality, a literary critic. We find him writing a letter to his friend Gaston, also a literary critic although masquerading *pro tem* as a guard at the Whitney Museum. Alphonse poises paws over his Smith-Corona and writes:

Dear Gaston,

Yes, you are absolutely right—Postmodernism is dead. A stunning blow, but not entirely surprising. I am spreading the news as rapidly as possible, so that all of our friends who are in the Postmodernist "bag" can get out of it before their cars are repossessed and the insurance companies tear up their policies. Sad to see Postmodernism go (and so quickly!). I was fond of it. As fond, almost, as I was of its grave and noble predecessor, Modernism. But we cannot dwell in the done-for. The death of a movement is a natural part of life, as was understood so well by the partisans of Naturalism, which is dead.

I remember exactly where I was when I realized that Postmodernism had bought it. I was in my study with a cup of tequila and William Y's new book, *One-Half*. Y's work is, we agree, good—*very* good. But who can make the leap to greatness while dragging after him the burnt-out boxcars of a dead aesthetic? Perhaps we can find new employment for him. On the roads, for example. When the insight overtook me, I started to my feet, knocking over the tequila, and said aloud (although there was no one to hear), "What? Postmodernism, too?" So many, so many. I put Y's book away on a high shelf and turned to the contemplation of the death of Plainsong, A.D. 958.

By the way: Structuralism's tottering. I heard it from Gerald, who is at Johns Hopkins and thus in the thick of things. You don't have to tell everybody. Frequently, idle talk is enough to give a movement that last little "push" that topples it into its grave. I'm convinced that's what happened to the New Criticism. I'm persuaded that it was Gerald, whispering in the corridors.

On the bright side, one thing that is dead that I don't feel too bad about is Existentialism, which I never thought was anything more than Phenomenology's bathwater anyway. It had a good run, but how peeving it was to hear all those artists going around talking about "the existential moment" and similar claptrap. Luckily, they have stopped doing that now. Similarly, the Nouveau Roman's passing did not disturb me overmuch. "Made dreariness into a religion," you said, quite correctly. I know this was one of your pared-to-the-bone movements and all that, but I didn't even like what they left out. A neat omission usually raises the hairs on the back of my neck. Not here. Robbe-Grillet's only true success, for my money, was with *Jealousy,* which I'm told he wrote in a fit of.

Well, where are we? Surrealism gone, got a little sweet toward the end, you could watch the wine of life turning into Gatorade. Sticky. Altar Poems—those constructed in the shape of an altar for the greater honor and glory of God—have not been seen much lately: missing and presumed dead. The Anti-Novel is dead; I read it in the *Times.* The Anti-Hero and the Anti-Heroine had a thing going which resulted in three Anti-Children, all of them now at M.I.T. The Novel of the Soil is dead, as are Expressionism, Impressionism, Futurism, Imagism, Vorticism, Regionalism, Realism, the Kitchen Sink School of Drama, the Theatre of the Absurd, the Theatre of Cruelty, Black Humor, and Gongorism. You know all this; I'm just totting up. To be a Pre-Raphaelite in the present era is to be somewhat out of touch. And, of course, Concrete Poetry—sank like a stone.

So we have a difficulty. What shall we call the New Thing, which I haven't encountered yet but which is bound to be out there somewhere? Post-Postmodernism sounds, to me, a little lumpy. I've been toying with the Revolution of the Word, II, or the New Revolution of the Word, but I'm afraid the Jolas estate may hold a copyright. It should have the word *new* in it somewhere. The New Newness? Or maybe the Post-New? It's a problem. I await your comments and suggestions. If we're going to slap a saddle on this rough beast, we've got to get moving.

Yours,
Alphonse

If I am slightly more sanguine than Alphonse about Post-modernism, however dubious about the term itself and not altogether clear as to who is supposed to be on the bus and who is not, it's because I locate it in relation to a series of problems, and feel that the problems are durable ones. Problems are a comfort. [Linguistic theorist Ludwig] Wittgenstein said, of philosophers, that some of them suffer from "loss of problems," a development in which everything seems quite simple to them and what they write becomes "immeasurably shallow and trivial." The same can be said of writers. Before I mention some of the specific difficulties I have in mind, I'd like to at least glance at some of the criticisms that have been leveled at the alleged Postmodernists— let's say John Barth, William Gass, John Hawkes, Robert Coover, William Gaddis, Thomas Pynchon, and myself in this country, Calvino in Italy, Peter Handke and Thomas Bernhard in Germany, although other names could be invoked. The criticisms run roughly as follows: that this kind of writing has turned its back on the world, is in some sense not about the world but about its own processes, that it is masturbatory, certainly chilly, that it excludes readers by design, speaks only to the already tenured, or that it does not speak at all, but instead, like [Robert] Frost's Secret, sits in the center of a ring and Knows.

PROBLEMS FACING THE POSTMODERNIST AUTHOR

I would ardently contest each of these propositions, but it's rather easy to see what gives rise to them. The problems that seem to me to define the writer's task at this moment (to the extent that he has chosen them as his problems) are not of a kind that make for ease of communication, for work that rushes toward the reader with outflung arms—rather, they're the reverse. Let me cite three such difficulties that I take to be important, all having to do with language. First, there is art's own project, since [poet Stéphane] Mallarmé, of restoring freshness to a much-handled language, essentially an effort toward finding a language in which making art is possible at all. This remains a ground theme, as potent, problematically, today as it was a century ago. Secondly, there is the political and social contamination of language by its use in manipulation of various kinds over time and the effort to find what might be called a "clean" language, problems associated with the Roland Barthes of *Writing Degree*

Zero but also discussed by [marxist literary theorist Georg] Lukács and others. Finally, there is the pressure on language from contemporary culture in the broadest sense—I mean our devouring commercial culture—which results in a double impoverishment: theft of complexity from the reader, theft of the reader from the writer.

These are by no means the only thorny matters with which the writer has to deal, nor (allowing for the very great differences among the practitioners under discussion) does every writer called Postmodern respond to them in the same way and to the same degree, nor is it the case that other writers of quite different tendencies are innocent of these concerns. If I call these matters "thorny," it's because any adequate attempt to deal with them automatically creates barriers to the ready assimilation of the work. Art is not difficult because it wishes to be difficult, but because it wishes to be art. However much the writer might long to be, in his work, simple, honest, and straightforward, these virtues are no longer available to him. He discovers that in being simple, honest, and straightforward, nothing much happens: he speaks the speakable, whereas what we are looking for is the as-yet unspeakable, the as-yet unspoken. . . .

Problems in part define the kind of work the writer chooses to do, and are not to be avoided but embraced. A writer, says Karl Kraus, is a man who can make a riddle out of an answer.

Let me begin again.

Jacqueline and Jemima are instructing Zeno, who has returned the purloined GRE documents and is thus restored to dull respectability, in Postmodernism. Postmodernism, they tell him, has turned its back on the world, is not about the world but about its own processes, is masturbatory, certainly chilly, excludes readers by design, speaks only to the already tenured, or does not speak at all, but instead—

Zeno, to demonstrate that he too knows a thing or two, quotes the critic Perry Meisel on semiotics. "Semiotics," he says, "is in a position to claim that no phenomenon has any ontological status outside its place in the particular information system from which it draws its meaning"—he takes a large gulp of his Gibson—"and therefore, all language is finally groundless." I am eavesdropping and I am much reassured. This insight is one I can use. Gaston, the critic who is a guard at the Whitney Museum, is in love with an IRS agent named Madelaine, the very IRS agent, in fact, who is auditing my return for the year 1982. "Madelaine," I say kindly to her over lunch, "semiotics is in a position to claim that no phenomenon has any ontological status outside its place in the particular information system from which it draws its meaning, and therefore, all language is finally groundless, including that of those funny little notices you've been sending me." "Yes," says Madelaine kindly, pulling from her pocket a large gold pocket watch that Alphonse has sold Gaston for twenty dollars, her lovely violet eyes atwitter, "but some information systems are more enforceable than others." Alas, she's right.

If the writer is taken to be the work's way of getting itself written, a sort of lightning rod for an accumulation of atmospheric disturbances, a St. Sebastian absorbing in his tattered breast the arrows of the Zeitgeist, this changes not very much the traditional view of the artist. But it does license a very great deal of critical imperialism.

This is fun for everyone. A couple of years ago I received a letter from a critic requesting permission to reprint a story of mine as an addendum to the piece he had written about it. He attached the copy of my story he proposed to reproduce, and I was amazed to find that my poor story had sprouted a set of tiny numbers—one to eighty-eight, as I recall—an army of tiny numbers marching over the surface of my poor distracted text. Resisting the temptation to tell him that all the tiny numbers were in the wrong places, I gave him permission to do what he wished, but I did notice that by a species of literary judo the status of my text had been reduced to that of footnote. . . .

Modern-day critics speak of "recuperating" a text, suggesting an accelerated and possibly strenuous nursing back to health of a basically sickly text, very likely one that did not even know itself to be ill. I would argue that in the competing methodologies of contemporary criticism, many of them quite rich in implications, a sort of tyranny of great expectations obtains, a rage for final explanations, a refusal to allow a work that mystery which is essential to it. I hope I am not myself engaging in mystification if I say, not that the attempt should not be made, but that the mystery exists. I see no immediate way out of the paradox—tear a mystery to tatters and you have tatters, not mystery—I merely note it and pass on.

Chapter 2

Types of Postmodernism

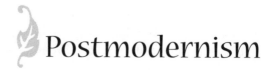
Postmodernism

The Tragic View of Categories

John Barth

Since the publication of his 1968 essay "The Literature of Exhaustion," John Barth has been intrinsically involved with the conception of postmodernism in the minds of writers and readers alike. He is the author of ten novels and several books of stories and essays as well as professor emeritus of English at Johns Hopkins University. The excerpt below is taken from Barth's 1988 essay "Postmodernism Revisited," the third in a series of pieces that spans two decades. Beginning with "The Literature of Exhaustion" and moving through "The Literature of Replenishment" in 1979 and the essay from which this selection is taken, Barth consistently worked toward finding an understanding of the postmodern label so often applied to his work. Here he begins discussing the tendency for humans to place things into categories and grudgingly accepts the need to do so. He follows this by listing the various categories into which he has been placed throughout his career, often with a sense of puzzlement as to what they meant. He ultimately argues that only one category really holds his interest in describing literature, namely whether or not a work is "terrific."

Perhaps because I'm a novelist by trade, I am by temperament much more Aristotelian than Platonist in my attitude toward reality: more nominalist than realist, especially as regards human beings and the things they do and make. Fred and Shirley and Mike and Irma seem intuitively realer to me than does the category *human beings;* the cathedrals at Seville and Barcelona and Santiago de Compostela strike me as more substantial than the term *Spanish Gothic;* and the writings of Gabriel García Márquez and Italo Calvino and Salman Rushdie and Thomas Pynchon—even the writings of John Barth—have ontological primacy, to my way of thinking, over the category *Postmodernist fiction.* To me it seems self-evident (although I know very well that it is not) that *this* rose and *that* rose and *that* rose—Fred, Irma, and Shirley Rose—are real items in the world, whereas the term *rose* names an idea in our minds, a generality that we achieve only by ignoring enough particularity; and further, that such generalities, while not necessarily illusions, are of an order of reality secondary to that of individual roses. In my innocent universe, in short, classes of objects are not *un*-real, but they're less real than their members.

CATEGORIZING

On the other hand, categories and similar abstractions, such as common nouns themselves, although they are (to my way of thinking) more or less fictions, are nevertheless indispensable fictions: indispensable to thought and discourse, to cognition and comprehension, even to sanity. How blithely I have divided reality already, in just a couple of paragraphs, into Aristotelians and Platonists, classes and members, novelists and cathedrals and roses and paragraphs and human beings, like a fisherman culling his catch. How glibly I deploy even such a fishy fiction as the pronoun *I,* as if—although more than half of the cells of my physical body replace themselves in the time it takes me to write one book (and I've written ten), and I've forgotten much more than I remember about my childhood, and the fellow who did things under my name forty years ago seems as alien to me now in many ways as an extraterrestrial—as if despite those considerations there really is an apprehensible antecedent to the first person singular pronoun. It is a far-fetched fiction indeed, as David Hume pointed out 250 years ago; but if I did not presume and act upon it, not only would I go insane; I'd be insane.

This is the Tragic View of Categories. Terms like Romanticism, Modernism, and Postmodernism are more or less useful and necessary fictions: roughly approximate maps, more likely to lead us to something like a destination if we don't confuse them with what they're meant to be maps of. . . .

We have arrived at Postmodernism, which is where I came in a couple of decades ago. More exactly, my first visits to that mildly vexed subject were two little essays written between novels: "The Literature of Exhaustion" (1968) and "The Literature of Replenishment" (1979). If my approach here to a revisit has been particularly tentative and crabwise, that is because my experience with the term and with the various phenomena that it has been used to name has been similarly so. I shall review now that experience: my personal and particular interest in Postmodernism beyond my general interest, as a sentient citizen, in understanding what's going on around me: what my artistic predecessors, contemporaries, and successors have been and are up to.

JOHN BARTH'S CAREER IN CATEGORIES

The writer of these words is a fifty-eight-year-old storyteller, mainly a novelist, who—as a student in the 1940s and Fifties—cut his apprentice literary teeth on the likes of Franz Kafka, Thomas Mann, James Joyce, T.S. Eliot, and Ezra Pound: the old masters of what we now call literary High Modernism, as that last term is understood in many parts of the world.

When my first novel *(The Floating Opera)* was published in the mid-1950s, it was approved by the critic Leslie Fiedler as an example of "provincial American existentialism." The description intrigued me; like a good provincial, I went and read Sartre and Camus to learn what Existentialism was, and I concurred with Mr. Fiedler (who later became a colleague and friend), if not altogether with Sartre and Camus. If people had done such things in those days, I'd have had a T-shirt printed up for myself: PROVINCIAL AMERICAN EXISTENTIALIST.

My second novel—*The End of the Road,* published two years later—was generally assigned to a new category called Black Humor. I buckled down and read such alleged fellow Black Humorists as John Hawkes, Kurt Vonnegut, Bruce Jay Friedman, and (when he arrived on the scene) Joseph Heller, and I decided that this was not a bad team to be on: the Existential Black Humorists.

But my third, fourth, and fifth books,. published through the 1960s, came to be described no longer as Existentialist or Black Humorist, but as Fabulist, and the term was made retroactive to those earlier productions too, as well as to the fiction of John Hawkes again and now of Donald Barthelme, Robert Coover, Stanley Elkin, William Gass, and Thomas Pynchon, to name only some of my new (and old) teammates. As before, I dutifully did my homework: read up on those of my fellow Fabulists with whom I wasn't already familiar, and decided that I liked that term—and that team—even better than I had liked its predecessors. But of course I went right on doing what it seemed to me I'd always done: not particularly thinking in terms of Existentialism, Black Humor, or Fabulism, but putting this sentence after that one, and the next one after this one.

Sure enough, just when I had got a pretty good idea what Fabulism was, in the 1970s the stuff began to be called Postmodernist. With increasing frequency I found myself categorized under that label, not only with my old U.S. teammates but with some first-rate foreign ones: Samuel Beckett, Jorge Luis Borges, Italo Calvino, Gabriel García Márquez. I had hoped that some women would sign on next time the ship changed names—would *be signed on*, I should say, since the artists themselves are not normally consulted in these matters. In any case, the crew was certainly strengthened by those world-class additions. But what exactly were the critics referring to?

SEEKING THE POSTMODERN

You will understand that by this time I found that familiar question less than urgent. All the same, it interested me that those who used the term "Postmodern," at least with respect to literature, seemed far less in agreement about its reference than had the users of labels like Fabulist and Black Humorist. If Joyce was a Modernist, was Beckett then a Postmodernist? Indeed, if the Joyce of *Ulysses* was a Modernist, had the Joyce of *Finnegans Wake* already moved on to Postmodernism? Was Laurence Sterne's *Tristram Shandy* proto-Modern or proto-Postmodern? More important, was the whole phenomenon, whatever it was, no more than a pallid ghost of the powerful cultural force that international Modernism had been in the first half of this century, or was it a positive new direction in the old art of storytelling, and in other arts as well? Was it a repudiation of the great Modernists at whose figurative feet I had sat, or was it something evolved out of them, some next stage of the ongoing dialectic between artistic generations that has characterized Western Civ at least since the advent of Romanticism in (I'm going to say) the latter eighteenth century?

My opportunity to find out came at the close of the

decade. The *Deutsche Gesellschaft für Amerikastudien,* an association of German professors of American subjects, convenes annually at Whitsuntide in one or another of that nation's universities, as our Modern Language Association does between Christmas and New Year's in one or another of our Hilton hotels. In 1979 the Gesellschaft took as the general subject of its conference "America in the 1970s," and the Literature section chose as its particular topic "Postmodern American Fiction." Three U.S. writers—William Gass, John Hawkes, and myself—were invited to Tübingen as guests of the conference, a kind of live exhibit. By that time the term really had gained wide currency in literature as well as in architecture and painting; I even had a rough idea how it might be applied to what was going on in my own shop. But when I looked over some of the standard critical texts (faithfully doing my homework again), I was surprised to find that although the century was 79 percent expired, there was still considerable disagreement about what "Modernism" means, or meant, not to mention Postmodernism, about which no two authorities seemed to agree.

Therefore I leaped into the breach—rather, I sidled crabwise into it—and drafted a little talk for the Gesellschaft on what I thought the term *ought* to mean, if it was going to describe anything very good very well. Armed with my tentative definition/prescription, I went off to Tübingen with my fellow former Fabulists Et Cetera, and found to my mild dismay that our German hosts, the object of whose meticulous curiosity we were, spoke of literary Postmodernism as if it were as indisputable a cultural-historical phenomenon as the Counter-Reformation or the Great Depression of the 1930s. Their discussion, and there was plenty, had to do with refining the boundaries and establishing the canon; there was so much confident bandying of adjectives and prefixes—High Postmodernism, Late Postmodernism, Proto-Postmodernism, Post-Postmodernism—that at the end of one session an American student remarked to me, "They forgot Post Toasties."

Moreover—perhaps on the principle that birds have no business holding forth on ornithology—our hospitable hosts weren't interested in hearing my lecture on their subject. My fellow exhibits and I read from our fiction instead, no doubt a sounder idea.

All the same, I had thought what I'd thought and I'd seen

what I'd said (to myself) on the subject of Postmodernist fiction. When I got home I published my reflections in *The Atlantic* (the monthly magazine, not the nearby ocean), where a dozen years before I had published some reflections on what I called "the literature of exhaustion." Here is the summarized conclusion of that Tübingen essay, "The Literature of Replenishment":

> If the Modernists, carrying the torch of Romanticism, taught us that linearity, rationality, consciousness, cause and effect, naive illusionism, transparent language, innocent anecdote, and middle-class moral conventions are not the whole story, then from the perspective of these closing decades of our century we may appreciate that the contraries of these things are not the whole story either. Disjunction, simultaneity, irrationalism, self-reflexiveness, medium-as-message, political olympianism . . . these are not the whole story either. . . .

> My ideal Postmodernist author neither merely repudiates nor merely imitates either his twentieth-century Modernist parents or his nineteenth-century premodernist grandparents. He has the first half of our century under his belt, but not on his back. Without lapsing into moral or artistic simplism, shoddy craftsmanship, Madison Avenue venality, or either false or real naiveté, he nevertheless aspires to a fiction more democratic in its appeal than such late-Modernist marvels as Beckett's *Texts for Nothing*. . . . The ideal Postmodernist novel will somehow rise above the quarrel between realism and irrealism, formalism and "contentism," pure and committed literature, coterie fiction and junk fiction. . . .

> What my [earlier] essay "The Literature of Exhaustion" was really about, so it seems to me now, was the effective "exhaustion" not of language or of literature but of the aesthetic of High Modernism: that admirable, not-to-be-repudiated, but essentially completed "program" of what Hugh Kenner has dubbed "the Pound era." In 1966/67 we scarcely had the term *Postmodernism* in its current literary-critical usage . . . but a number of us, in quite different ways and with varying combinations of intuitive response and conscious deliberation, were already well into the working out, not of the next-best thing after Modernism, but of the *best next* thing: what is gropingly now called Postmodernist fiction. . . .

Et cetera: There is more to the definition and more to the argument, but that's the general idea.

Postmodernism as of the Late 1980s

Now, then: The difference between professional intellectuals and professional artists who are perhaps amateur intellectuals is that the former publish articles and essays in order to share their learning, whereas we latter may publish the odd essay-between-novels in order to share our ignorance, so that those more learned can come to our rescue. My little essay on Postmodernism has been translated and reprinted a number of times over the years since its first publication, and my rescuers have been many. Although I still hold to my basic notion of what Postmodernist fiction is—or ought to be if it's to deserve our attention—I have happily withdrawn from the ongoing disputes over its definition and its canon: over who should be admitted into the club or (depending on the critic's point of view) clubbed into admission. Postmodern, I tell myself serenely, is what I am; ergo, Postmodernism is whatever I do, together with my crewmates-this-time-around, until the critics rename the boat again. Moreover, *it is what I do whether I do it well or badly:* a much more important critical consideration, to which I shall return.

But as I go on doing it, I note with respect and mild interest observations on the subject made by my peers and betters. Octavio Paz, in the Mexican literary organ *La Jornada Semanal,* declared huffily that since I've got *el modernismo* all wrong (that special Hispanic distinction again), I can scarcely be trusted with *el post-modernismo,* which anyhow he was already writing about decades ago, under a different term, as I would have known were I not just one more gringo ethnocentric. There's a rescuer for you. The writers whom I call Postmodernist, Susan Sontag and William Gass call Late Modernist; for them, the American Postmoderns are the minimalist-realists of the 1970s and Eighties: Raymond Carver, Ann Beattie, and company. The Australian-American art critic Robert Hughes dates Postmodernism, at least in its Pop Art manifestation, from that moment in Walt Disney's 1940 movie *Fantasia* when Mickey Mouse mounts the conductor's podium and shakes hands with Leopold Stokowski. I like that. But yet another art critic (and novelist), Tom McEvilly, speaks of an Egyptian postmodernism from the Middle Kingdom and a Roman postmodernism from the Silver Age; for McEvilly, lowercase postmodernism is the periodic swing of the pendulum of Western Civ from the spiritual-romantic (of which twentieth-century Modernism is an instance) toward the rational-skeptical. . . .

I'm interested too in the observation by the British architect Charles Jencks that whereas for Modernist artists the subject is often the *processes* of their medium, for Postmodernist artists it is more typically the *history* of their medium. On the basis of this distinction, Jencks classifies the Pompidou Center in Paris, for example, with its abstract patterns of boldly exposed and brightly painted pipes and trusses, as Late Modernist, and Robert Graham's Olympic Arch in Los Angeles—with its truncated classical nude bronze torsos balancing on inverted metal cones on a black granite dolmen like a streamlined ruin—as Postmodernist. But I'm not sure how far this interesting distinction carries over into literature. It is true that many of the writers called Postmodernist have looked to various sorts of myth for their material— whether classical myths or such pop mythologies as old Hollywood movies—as well as to premodern narrative forms, like the tale, the fable, and the gothic or the epistolary novel; also to premodern narrative devices, such as [José] Donoso's intrusive, commenting author. I've certainly made use of things like that. But then so did Joyce, in *Ulysses,* and if that benchmark of novelistic Modernism must be reclassified as Postmodernist, I for one begin to experience vertigo. I think I'll stick with Umberto Eco's "double coding"; in fact, think I'll stick with my own rough-and-ready definition of Postmodernism, quoted earlier. All the same, I recommend Charles Jencks's little treatise *What Is Post-Modernism?* (London/New York: Academy Editions/St. Martin's Press, 1986), an especially sound review of Postmodernist architecture, painting, and sculpture, with side glances at literature.

THE PENDULUM SWINGS

So how is literary Postmodernism doing these days, and what Post-Postmodernism, if any, lies around the next corner? In architecture, there seems to be no question that Postmodernism is where the action is, for better or worse. Almost nobody builds plain old International Style curtain-wall boxes anymore; even shopping malls have their ironic steel-and-glass gable ends, false fronts, cupolas, quotations from the Victorian, whatever. The style has triumphed, with the usual distribution of excellent, mediocre, and horrendous specimens that one finds in any established style. But although most of the leading practitioners of what is called Postmodernist fiction are by no means finished yet with their careers, and may feel themselves to be still in the process of defining the style (just as their critics are still defining and debating the term), it cannot be doubted that in (North) American fiction, at least, the pendulum has swung from the overtly self-conscious, process-*and*-history-conscious, and often fabulistic work of Barthelme, Coover, Elkin, Gass, Hawkes, Pynchon, & Co. toward that early-Hemingwayish minimalist neo-realism aforementioned, epitomized by the short stories of Carver, Beattie, Frederick Barthelme (the Houston Postmodernist Donald's next-younger brother), and others. Indeed, I suppose that just now these are the two main streams of contemporary U.S. fiction of the literary sort—fiction that, in Joseph Conrad's words, "aspires to the condition of art"—although there are many who would say that the best American work in the medium is being done by more "traditional" pigeons not usually associated with either of these holes: writers such as Saul Bellow, Norman Mailer, Joyce Carol Oates, William Styron, Anne Tyler, John Updike. That may be.

In any case (back to my starting point), be it remembered that the question whether a particular novel or painting or building is Late Modernist, Postmodernist, Post-Postmodernist, or none of the above, while it's not an unworthy question, is of less importance—at least it ought to be so—than the question *Is it terrific?*

In this connection, it's worth remarking that in literature, at least, an artist may be historically notable without being especially good (for this reader, Theodore Dreiser is one such, Gertrude Stein another; others will have other examples). Conversely, a writer may be quite good without being otherwise especially "important" (I think of the late Joyce Carey, of the late Henry Green, of others, not yet late, whom I shall not name). Alas, it is the misfortune of many, many published writers, perhaps of most, to be neither especially good nor particularly important; and it is the fortune of a very few to be both artistically excellent and historically significant. Since art is long and life short, *those* are the writers (if we can name them) to whom we ought to give our prime-time attention. Among our contemporaries, I quite believe, a few of these few are what has come to be called Postmodernist.

Surfiction: Writing with No Restraints

Raymond Federman

The terms "postmodern" and "experimental" have often been used synonymously in criticism of contemporary literature, a uniformity that Raymond Federman claims is false. Born in France in 1928, Federman was imprisoned during the Holocaust and emigrated to the United States in 1947. He subsequently took American citizenship and has become one of the most prominent American postmodern writers as well as a distinguished professor emeritus of English at SUNY-Buffalo. In this selection excerpted from a 1973 essay, he provides a manifesto for a new kind of fiction that he called "surfiction" (a blending of surrealism and fiction). Federman's "new" genre is based on the abolition of distinctions between such seemingly opposite pairs as reality and imagination, truth and untruth, or beauty and ugliness. He outlines four propositions for what he calls the "present-future" of fiction, all of which came true to some extent over the next twenty-five years.

Personally I do not believe that a fiction writer with the least amount of self-respect and integrity, and who believes in what he is doing, ever says to himself: "I am now going to write an experimental novel." Others say that about his work. It is the middleman, the procurer of literature (the failed novelist turned editor or journalist) who gives that label **EXPERIMENTAL** to what is unusual, difficult, innovative, provocative, intellectually challenging, and even original. In fact, true experiments (as in the sciences) never reach, or at least should never reach the printed page. A novel is always a form of experiment, and therefore becomes an experience. After all the two terms were synonymous at one time. Fiction is called experimental out of incomprehension and despair. It is those who are unwilling to give to a novel what it demands intellectually that declares that novel experimental. Samuel Beckett's novels are not experimental—no!—it is the only way he could write them; Jorge Luis Borges' stories are not experimental; Italo Calvino's fiction is not experimental; or going back in time to James Joyce or Franz Kafka, their fiction is not experimental (even though it was called that when it first appeared and is still called that by those who cannot accept what departs from the norm or refuses to submit to simple-mindedness). All these writers created successful and accomplished works of art that function on their own terms rather than on a set of predetermined rules.

DEFINING SURFICTION

And so, for me, the only fiction that still means something today is the kind of fiction that tries to explore the possibilities of fiction beyond its own limitations; the kind of fiction that challenges the tradition that governs it; the kind of fiction that constantly renews our faith in man's intelligence and imagination rather than man's distorted view of reality; the kind of fiction that reveals man's playful irrationality rather than his righteous rationality.

This I call **SURFICTION**. However, not because it imitates reality, but because it exposes the fictionality of reality. Just as the Surrealists called that level of man's experience that functions in the subconscious **SURREALITY**, I call that level of man's activity that reveals life as a fiction **SURFICTION**. In this sense there is some truth in the cliché that claims that "life imitates fiction," or that "life is like fiction," but not because of what is happening in the streets of our cities, but because reality as such does not exist, or rather exists only in its fictionalized version, that is to say in the language that describes it. . . .

Displacement, difference, and repetition, these are the givens of Surfiction, and no longer faithful imitation and truthful representation. Consequently, in the fiction of today and tomorrow, all distinctions between the real and the imaginary, between the conscious and the subconscious, between the past and the present, between truth and untruth will be abolished. All forms of duplicity will disappear. And above all, all forms of duality will be negated—yes, especially duality: that double-headed monster which for centuries subjected us to a system of ethical and aesthetical values based on the principles of good and bad, true and false, beautiful and ugly.

Surfiction will not be judged on such principles. It will neither be good nor bad, true nor false, beautiful nor ugly. It will simply **BE**, and its primary purpose will be to unmask its own fictionality, to expose the metaphor of its own fraudulence and simulacrum, and not pretend any longer to pass for reality, for truth, or for beauty.

As a result, Surfiction will no longer be regarded as a mirror of life, as a pseudorealistic document that informs us about life, nor will it be judged on the basis of its social, moral, psychological, metaphysical, or commercial value, but only on the basis of what it is and what it does as an autonomous art form in its own right—just as poetry, music or the plastic arts are autonomous.

These preliminary remarks serve as an introduction to four propositions I would now like to make for the present-future of fiction. These are but an arbitrary starting point for the possibilities of a New Fiction. Other positions and other propositions are possible. My propositions will be dogmatic, but that's how it should be, because this text is in fact a manifesto for Surfiction, and as such it can only be dogmatic. One accepts or rejects a manifesto in its entirety, but one cannot argue with it. . . .

PROPOSITION ONE—THE READING OF FICTION

The very act of reading a book, starting at the top of the first page, and moving from left to right, top to bottom, page after page to the end in a consecutive prearranged manner has become *restrictive and boring*. Indeed, any intelligent reader should feel frustrated and restricted within that preordained system of reading.

Therefore, the whole traditional, conventional, fixed, and boring method of reading a book must be questioned, challenged, and demolished. And it is the writer (and not modern printing technology alone) who must, through innovations in the writing itself—in the typography of the text and the topography of the book—renew our system of reading.

All the rules and principles of printing and bookmaking must be forced to change as a result of the changes in the writing (or the telling) of a story in order to give the reader a sense of free participation in the writing/reading process, in order to give the reader an element of choice (active choice) in the ordering of the discourse and the discovery of its meaning.

Thus the very concept of syntax must be transformed. Syntax, traditionally, is the unity, the continuity of words, the law that dominates them. Syntax reduces the multiplicity of words and controls their energy and their violence. It fixes words into a place, a space, and prescribes an order to them. It prevents words from wandering. Even if it is hidden, syntax always reigns on the horizon of words which buckle under its mute exigency.

Therefore, words, sentences, paragraphs (and of course the punctuation) and their position on the page and in the book must be rethought and rewritten so that new ways (multiple and simultaneous ways) of reading these can be created. And even the typographical design of the pages and the numbering of these pages must be reinvented. The space itself in which writing takes place must be transformed. That space—the page, but also the book made of pages—must acquire new dimensions, new shapes, new relations in order to accommodate the new writing. Pages no longer need to be the same uniform rectangular size, and books no longer need to be rectangular boxes. It is within this transformed topography of writing, from this new **paginal syntax** rather than **grammatical syntax** that the reader will discover his freedom in relation to the process of reading a book, in relation to language.

In all other art forms there are always three essential elements at play: the creator who fabricates the work of art, the medium through which the work of art is transmitted, and the receiver (listener or viewer) to whom the work of art is transmitted. It seems that in the writing of fiction only the first and the third elements are at work: the writer and the reader. Me and you. And the medium—and by medium I do not mean the story or the mental cinema one plays while reading fiction, but the language itself—is forgotten. It becomes absent, or rather it is absented, negated by the process of reading, as if it were transparent, as if it were there only to carry the reader into the realm of illusions. Is it because while reading fiction one does not think of the language as being auditory or visual (as in music, painting, and even poetry) that it merely serves as a means of transportation from the author to the reader? From me to you, from what I supposedly meant to what you supposedly understand of my meaning? This obsolete form of reading devaluates the medium of fiction, reduces language to a mere function.

If we are to make of the novel an art form, we must raise the printed word as the medium, and therefore **where** and **how** it is placed on the page makes a difference in what the fiction will be for the reader. In other words, we as fiction writers must render language concrete and visible so that it will be more than just a functional thing that supposedly reflects reality. Thus, not only the writer will create the fiction, but all those involved in the producing and ordering of that fiction; the typist, the editor, the typesetter, the printer, the proofreader, and of course the reader will all partake of the fiction. The real medium will be the printed words as they are presented on the page, as they are perceived, heard, visualized (not abstractly but concretely), as they are read by all those involved in the making of the book.

PROPOSITION TWO—THE SHAPE OF FICTION

If life and fiction are no longer distinguishable one from the other, nor complementary to one another, and if we agree that life is never linear, that in fact life is always discontinuous and chaotic because it is never experienced in a straight line or an orderly fashion, then similarly linear, chronological, and sequential narration is no longer possible.

The pseudorealistic novel sought to give a semblance of order to the chaos of life, and did so by relying on the well-made plot (the story line as it was called) which, as we now realize, has become quite inessential to fiction. The plot having disappeared, it is no longer necessary to have the events of fiction follow a linear, sequential pattern in time and space. Nor is it necessary for the narrative to obey logical transitions, or be controlled by a system of cause and effect.

Therefore, the elements of the surfictional discourse (words, phrases, sequences, scenes, spaces, word-designs, sections, chapters, etc.) must become digressive from one another—digressive from the element that precedes and the element that follows. In fact, these elements will not only wander freely in the book and even be repeated, but in some places they will occur simultaneously. This will offer multiple possibilities of rearrangement in the process of reading.

No longer progressing from left to right, top to bottom, in a straight line, and along the design of an imposed plot, the surfictional discourse will follow the contours of the writing itself as it takes shape (unpredictable shape) within the space of the page. In other words, as it improvises itself, the surfictional discourse will circle around itself, create new and unexpected movements and figures in the unfolding of the narration, repeating itself, projecting itself backward and forward along the curves of the writing—(much here can be learned from the cinema, or experiments in the visual arts).

As a result of the improvisational quality of language in this process, the events related in the narration will also unfold along unexpected and unpredictable lines. The shape and order of the story will not result from an imitation of the artificial shape and order of life, but from the formal circumvolutions of language as it wells up from the unconscious.

No longer acting as a mirror being dragged along the path of reality, Surfiction will now reproduce the effects of the mirror acting upon itself. It will not be a representation of something exterior to it, it will be a self-representation. Surfiction will be self-reflexive. That is to say, rather than being the stable image of daily life, Surfiction will be in a perpetual state of redoubling upon itself in order to disclose its own life—THE LIFE OF FICTION. It will be from itself, from its own substance that Surfiction will proliferate—imitating, repeating, echoing, parodying, mocking, re-tracing what it will say. Thus fiction will become the metaphor of its own narrative progress, and will establish and generate itself as it writes itself.

This does not mean, however, that the future novel will only be a *novel of the novel,* but rather it will create a kind of writing, a kind of discourse whose shape will be an interrogation, an endless interrogation of what it is doing while doing it, but also a relentless denunciation of its own fraudulence, of what **IT** really **IS**: an illusion (a fiction), just as life is an illusion (a fiction).

PROPOSITION THREE—THE MATERIAL OF FICTION

If the experiences of a human being (in this case those of the writer) occur only as fiction, gain meaning only as they are recalled or recounted, afterwards, and always in a distorted, glorified, sublimated manner, then these experiences become inventions. And if most fiction is based (more or less) on the experiences of the one who writes (experiences that are not necessarily anterior to, but simultaneous with, the writing process), there cannot be any truth nor any reality exterior to fiction. In other words, if the material of fiction is invention (lies, simulations, affectations, distortions, exaggerations, illusions), then writing fiction will be a process of fabricating or improvising on the spot the material of fiction.

The writer will simply materialize (render concrete) experiences into words. As such there will be no limits to the material of fiction—no limits beyond the writer's power of imagination, and beyond the possibilities of language.

Everything can be said and must be said in any possible way. While pretending to be telling the story of his life, or the life story of some imaginary being, the surfictionist can at the same time tell the story of the story he is in the process of inventing, he can tell the story of the language he is using, he can tell the story of the pencil or the typewriter or whatever instrument or machine he is using to write the story he is making up as he goes along, and he can also tell the story of the anguish or joy, disgust or exhilaration he is feeling while writing his story.

Since writing means filling a space (blackening pages), in those spaces where there is nothing to write, the writer can, at any time, introduce material (quotations, pictures, charts, diagrams, designs, illustrations, doodles, lists, pieces of other discourses, etc.) totally unrelated to the story he is in the process of inventing. Or else he can simply leave those spaces blank, because fiction is as much what is said as what is not said, since what is said is not necessarily true, and since what is said can always be said another way. There is no constriction in the writing of fiction, only arbitrariness and freedom.

As a result, the people of fiction, the fictitious beings will no longer be called characters, well-made characters who carry with them a fixed personality, a stable set of social and psychological attributes (a name, a gender, a condition, a profession, a situation, a civic identity). These surfictional creatures will be as changeable, as volatile, as irrational, as nameless, as *unnamable,* as playful, as unpredictable, as fraudulent and frivolous as the discourse that makes them. This does not mean, however, that they will be mere puppets. On the contrary, their being will be more complex, more genuine, more authentic, more true to life in fact, because (since life and fiction are no longer distinguishable) they will not appear to be what they are: imitations of real people; they will be what they are: word-beings.

What will replace the well-made personage (the hero, the protagonist) of traditional fiction who carried with him the burden of a name, an age, parental ties, a social role, a nationality, a past, and sometimes a physical appearance and even an interior psyche, will be a creation, or better yet a creature that will function outside any predetermined conditions of society, outside any precise moment of history. That creature will be, in a sense, present to its own making, present also to its own unmaking. The surfictional being will not be a man or a woman of a certain moment, it will be the language of humanity. Totally free, arbitrary, and disengaged, uncommitted to the affairs of the outside world to the same extent as the fictitious discourse in which it will exist, this creature will participate in the fiction only as a grammatical being (in some cases devoid of a pronominal referent). Made of linguistic fragments often disassociated from one another, this word-being will be irrepressive, amoral, irrational and irresponsible in the sense that it will be detached from the real world, but entirely committed to the fiction in which it will find itself, aware only of the role it has to play as a fictional element.

Since Surfiction will no longer offer itself as a social or historical document that informs the reader about **real life** and **real people**, but as a work of art that functions on its own terms, the reader will no longer be tempted to identify with the characters. Instead the reader will participate in the creation of the fiction in the same degree as the creator or the narrator or the creature of that fiction. All of them will be part of the fictional discourse, all of them will be responsible for it. The writer just as (fictitious as his creation) will only be the point of junction (the source and the recipient) of all the elements of fiction. The story that he will be writing will also write him, just as it will write the reader who gives meaning to the story as he reads it.

PROPOSITION FOUR—THE MEANING OF FICTION

It is evident from the preceding propositions that the most striking and most radical aspects of Surfiction will be its semblance of disorder and its deliberate incoherency. Since, as stated earlier, no meaning preexists language, but meaning is produced in the process of writing and reading, Surfiction will not attempt to be meaningful, truthful, or realistic, *a priori;* nor will it serve as the vehicle of a ready-made sense. On the contrary, Surfiction will be seemingly devoid of meaning, it will be deliberately illogical, irrational, irrealistic, non sequitur, digressive, and incoherent. And of course, since the surfictional story will not have a beginning, middle, and end, it will not lend itself to a continuous and totalizing form of reading. It will refuse resolution and closure. It will always remain an open discourse—a discourse open to multiple interpretations. Surfiction will not only be the product of imagination, it will also activate imagination. For it will be through the collective efforts of all those who participate in the fiction (author, narrator, fictitious being, reader) that a meaning will be formulated. Surfiction will not create a semblance of order, it will offer itself for order and ordering. Thus the reader will not be able to identify with the people or the situations, nor will he be able to purify or purge himself in relation to the actions of the people in the story. In other words, no longer manipulated by an authorial (and authoritarian) point of view, no longer entrapped into the suspension of credibility, the reader will be the one who extracts, invents, creates an order and a meaning for the creatures and the material of fiction. It is this total and free participation in the fiction that will give the reader the sense of having invented a meaning, and not simply having passively received a neatly prearranged meaning.

As for the writer, he will no longer be considered a seer, a prophet, a theologian, a philosopher, or even a sociologist who predicts, preaches, teaches, or reveals absolute truths. Nor will he be looked upon (admiringly and romantically) as an omnipresent, omniscient, omnipotent creator. He will simply stand on equal footing with the reader in their efforts **to make sense** out of a language common to both of them— their collective efforts **to give sense** to the fiction of life. In other words, as it has been said of poetry, fiction will also **BE** and not only **MEAN.**

"Cyberpunk" as a Branch of Postmodernism

Joseph Tabbi

Since the mid-1980s, a subset of postmodernist writing has developed in the United States. Called "cyberpunk" literature due to both its fascination with technology and its anti-authoritarian tendencies, this genre has been popularized by writers like William Gibson, Raymond Federman, Bruce Sterling, Neal Stephenson, and others. Joseph Tabbi, assistant professor of English at the University of Illinois-Chicago, provides a brief history of cyberpunk's development as well as an analysis of some of the ways in which this genre is a modification of ideas popularized by more mainstream writers generally associated with postmodernism. For example, Tabbi argues that cyberpunk's obsession with the role of an individual in an impersonal society (often called "the machine" or "the system") and its pessimism are closely affiliated with postmodernism in general, but that its emphasis on marginalized "heroes" is somewhat unusual.

As we have advanced from a post–World War II period of expanding technological potential to a period of practical consequences, we are witnessing material actualizations even vaster, though probably less exciting, than those imagined in literature. The corporate and political world itself, says Siemion, has had "no place or use for infinitely accurate, infinitely demanding, non-traditional communications" of the sort considered here (private correspondence). Mainstream authors who have continued to work the technological terrain staked out in the sixties and not mined to exhaustion in the seventies and early eighties have increasingly bypassed the details of technological operations in favor of their simulations. Instead of the conceptual naturalism and experimental exuberance such details inspired in [Thomas] Pynchon, [Joseph] McElroy, [Don] DeLillo, [Robert] Coover, and [William] Gaddis, we are now offered, in Siemion's words, "the synthetic, simulated vistas of William Gibson's *Neuromancer.*"

The so-called cyberpunk fiction of the eighties and nineties clearly owes a debt to postmodernist literary experiments of the preceding decades. Raymond Federman lists McElroy's *Plus,* Pynchon's *Gravity's Rainbow,* and DeLillo's *Ratner's Star* as obvious precursors, along with works such as Samuel Beckett's *Lost Ones,* Russell Hoban's *Riddley Walker,* Federman's own *Twofold Vibration,* and Italo Calvino's *Cosmicomics* and *T/Zero,* which have not been discussed here, but which might be included among those self-conscious, often cerebral tours de force that posit fiction as primarily a growth of language. Without these books, notes Federman, "there wouldn't be any Cyberpunk Fiction." Federman, however, wrongly accuses his younger peers of failing to give credit where credit is due, and of much else besides, evincing a resentment that is, I would guess, the surprise of a pure postmodern experimentalist and programmatic antirealist at the practical realization of an a priori [self-evident] project. The difference between cyberpunk and its postmodern textualist predecessors is the difference, in the aesthetic sphere, between paper science and lab science, ideal and practical reason, the material advance of current computer technologies and the previous generation's heady theory.

Gibson himself takes the edge off such discussions by blithely acknowledging his literary antecedents, but without according them any greater influence than that of artists working in other media. He says, "I've been influenced by [musician] Lou Reed, for instance, as much as I've been by any 'fiction' writer." Even more encompassing is Bruce Sterling's announcement, in his definitive preface to the *Mirrorshades* collection, of "a new kind of integration. The overlapping of worlds that were formerly separate: the realm of high tech and the modern pop underground." Federman had accused cyberpunk of not being explicit about just *what* was being newly integrated, but the consequences of the previous generation's experimentation reveal themselves quite clearly in this quotation: in an era of literary exhaustion and market saturation, possibilities might still expand and growth continue—in aesthetics no less than in economics—through hybridization, the corporate merger, the fluidity of seemingly inexhaustible connections across media and genres that are themselves perceived as defunct.

The cyberpunk writer thus typically sees himself (and until work by Pat Cadigan and Marge Piercy, cyberpunk had been, like its postmodern precursors in technology and literature, mostly a male genre) as leveling distinctions between the technical and the literary, fiction and history, "high" and "popular" cultures. This generic flexibility, while generally seen to characterize cyberpunk's postmodernism, is also a feature of the sublime moment in both modernist and romantic literature. At least since Wordsworth the sublime has always "brought the high and the low into dangerous proximity"; it "will always be found in the ill-defined zones of anxiety between discrete orders of meaning." In order for the hybrid narrative to *be* sublime, however, the "discrete orders" must be kept clear and separate. As Brian McHale points out in *Constructing Postmodernism,* the "high culture/low culture distinction" in particular, like the "Difference Engine" that provides the title of Gibson's and Sterling's one collaborative work, may well be necessary, "in however problematic or attenuated a form," in order for "the cultural engine to continue to turn over."

CYBERPUNK: A HYPERSPEED FORM OF POSTMODERNISM

McHale finds the cultural cross-fertilization in cyberpunk to be a characteristic as much of modernism as of postmodernism, but where the two may diverge is in the "technologically-enhanced speed of the traffic in models between the high and low strata of culture." The postmodernist desire has been to erase the categorical distinctions that earlier forms of the sublime have traditionally depended upon. And nowhere is the loss of traditional distinctions more apparent than in cyberpunk's flattened conception of character and identity. The ultimate a posteriori [derived from observation] criterion, once the last generation's highbrow productions are made operational and got ready for mass production, is functionality; and a new level of pragmatic functioning can be observed in cyberpunk's technological reconstitution of identity, what Gibson would call a "construct" or coded replication of a person's operational being. In *Neuromancer,* for example, characters who have died frequently persist—if their skills are deemed by those in power important enough to preserve—as pure disembodied information that, in a Turing test, would answer to all we ever knew of the living person. (Alan Turing proposed as a thought experiment putting questions to a computer; if the answers given could be human, the machine could be considered intelligent.) A person's expertise, valued solely for its ability to negotiate the complexity of the corporate network, could itself be accessed solely through a piece of patented software on a computer disk. No other human characteristic is necessary, for consciousness itself is an autonomous function that does not need to be imagined as embodied in flesh and language at all.

THE QUINTESSENTIAL CYBERPUNK

Case, the hero of William Gibson's 1984 novel Neuromancer, *is a futuristic outlaw whose characterization is reminiscent of the "hard-boiled" characters popularized by Humphrey Bogart in films from the 1940s and '50s. Gibson also draws on the mood of Ridley Scott's 1982 film* Blade Runner *to create his postmodern setting, complete with technology, sex, narcotics, and popular culture elements from all over the world. Also, note Gibson's extensive use of unusual or even original words to set the tone of his story.*

Directly overhead, along the nighted axis, the hologram sky glittered with fanciful constellations suggesting playing cards, the faces of dice, a top hat, a martini glass. The intersection of Desiderata and Jules Verne formed a kind of gulch, the balconied terraces of Freeside cliff dwellers rising gradually to the grassy tablelands of another casino complex. Case watched a drone microlight bank gracefully in an updraft at the green verge of an artificial mesa, lit for seconds by the soft glow of the invisible casino. The thing was a kind of pilotless biplane of gossamer polymer, its wings silkscreened to resemble a giant butterfly. Then it was gone, beyond the mesa's edge. He'd seen a wink of reflected neon off glass, either lenses or the turrets of lasers. The drones were part of the spindle's security system, controlled by some central computer.

In Straylight? He walked on, past bars named the Hi-Lo, the Paradise, le Monde, Cricketeer, Shozoku Smith's, Emergency. He chose Emergency because it was the smallest and most crowded, but it took only seconds for him to realize that it was

Indeed, in *Neuromancer's* adolescent mysticism, immediate experience through the body is mostly "a meat thing" to be rejected in favor of the cerebral pleasures and the "consensual hallucination" of cyberspace, Gibson's figure for the entire global network of electronic communications. Anything less than participation in the network is experienced by the cyberpunk hero as a fall into materiality, into the dreary consumerist world. Yet this hero hardly manages to escape this culture by trivializing the body; his abstract, disembodied, and "unthinkably complex" consciousness is not romantic transcendence, but is rooted in the very culture of high-tech consumerism that enables Gibson to rewrite the body on the abstract space of corporate capital.

Its bodiless "data" are ultimately "made flesh in the mazes

a tourist place. No hum of biz here, only a glazed sexual tension. He thought briefly of the nameless club above Molly's rented cubicle, but the image of her mirrored eyes fixed on the little screen dissuaded him. What was Wintermute revealing there now? The ground plans of the Villa Straylight? The history of the Tessier-Ashpools?

He bought a mug of Carlsberg and found a place against the wall. Closing his eyes, he felt for the knot of rage, the pure small coal of his anger. It was there still. Where had it come from? He remembered feeling only a kind of bafflement at his maiming in Memphis, nothing at all when he'd killed to defend his dealing interests in Night City, and a slack sickness and loathing after Linda's death under the inflated dome. But no anger. Small and far away, on the mind's screen, a semblance of Deane struck a semblance of an office wall in an explosion of brains and blood. He knew then: the rage had come in the arcade, when Wintermute rescinded the simstim ghost of Linda Lee, yanking away the simple animal promise of food, warmth, a place to sleep. But he hadn't become aware of it until his exchange with the holo-construct of Lonny Zone.

It was a strange thing. He couldn't take its measure.

"Numb," he said. He'd been numb a long time, years. All his nights down Ninsei, his nights with Linda, numb in bed and numb at the cold sweating center of every drug deal. But now he'd found this warm thing, this chip of murder. *Meat,* some part of him said. *It's the meat talking, ignore it.*

William Gibson, *Neuromancer.* New York: Ace Books, 1984, pp. 151–53.

of the black market," and its "money," a nearly autonomous signifier that has separated itself from any indexical reference to material value, is used precisely to generate "a seamless universe of self."

From the moment of its appearance, cyberpunk could be all too easily recognized as an aesthetic suited to the excesses and economic hubris of the Reagan era; and during a decade when a much-hyped research program in "artificial intelligence" was at last delivering not a simulation of embodied consciousness but numerous expert systems of corporate organization and control, cyberpunk's presentation of character could just as easily be attacked as "unnatural." Nonetheless, like traditional liberal humanist criticisms of postmodern writers for not creating "round" characters, objections to the informatics of cyberpunk identity may be ultimately beside the point. Such characterizations might be best understood, I think, not only as the dystopian expression of a cultural narcissism or of the oncoming hegemony of the machine, but as a logical response to the crisis of representation I have mentioned. The prospect that identity might become wholly informational enables Gibson, like [Norman] Mailer, Pynchon, and their theorist contemporaries Fredric Jameson and Donna Haraway, to de-realize any notion of an individual and separate subject and thus to make identity itself an abstract representation of the vast and impersonal corporate networks that constitute so much of the contemporary life-world. As John Christie points out, Gibson, like Haraway, seems to have been "seduced by the possibilities of extending the technological sublime as the trope to figure out the political-aesthetic dimensions and possibilities of the infotech material formation."

"X Literature" and Post-Postmodern Literature

Daniel Grassian

As the twentieth century drew to a close, a number of younger writers—marked by their membership in the so-called "Generation X" (a term taken from the title of a novel by Douglas Coupland)—began to produce distinctly different literary works. Daniel Grassian, a doctoral candidate in English at the University of North Carolina at Chapel Hill, argues that the works of writers such as Coupland, Tama Janowitz, David Foster Wallace, and others can be grouped together under the banner of what he calls "X Literature". Grassian argues that their work is characterized by a return to realism (albeit, a form of realism corrupted by the absurdities of postmodern culture), heavy reliance on popular culture references and an emphasis on the individual in a superficial world. He also notes that X Literature has a great deal in common with American modernism as well as postmodernism.

Literary movements are often thought of in generational terms. Generationally affiliated writers are linked and shaped by a shared social and cultural background. The American modernists were largely defined by the disillusion brought on from the first World War and its aftermath. They also believed that their new form would literally, and literarily, save them. American postmodern writers are not traditionally affiliated with an American generation. However, most canonized American postmodernists are members of the Pre-War (also known as Silent) or Baby-Boomer generation (born primarily in the 1930's and 1940's). Their writing was influenced by the late 1950's and 1960's counter-cultural

Excerpted from *The Birth of X Literature: Generation X, Popular Culture, and American Literature*, by Daniel Grassian. Masters Thesis in the Department of English at the University of North Carolina. Copyright © 1999 Daniel Grassian. Reprinted with permission from the author.

defiance against the perceived social, political, and personal oppression of the elder "modernistic" generation. American postmodern writing was a form of literary rebellion in the radical spirit of this time to deconstruct the reigning literary, historical and philosophical aesthetics of the mythopoeic high modernists.

DOES GENERATION X HAVE ANY LITERATURE?

The American generation following the Baby Boomers is considered today as "Generation X," consisting of individuals born between 1960 and 1980. During the time that American postmodernism has been canonized (approximately the last fifteen or twenty years), a new literary genre has been developed primarily by Generation X writers, which has condescendingly been called Brat Pack fiction by established newspaper and magazine critics. Others have called the fiction of young contemporary writers anything from post-post modernism, image fiction, punk fiction, downtown writing, neo-realism, to minimalism. Literary critic James Annesley has recently published a book about contemporary American authors entitled *Blank Fictions* (1998). However, his portrait of contemporary fiction as preferring "blank, atonal perspectives, and fragile, glassy visions," is a gross generalization that carries a derogatory connotation of insubstantiality. Because of the apparent inability to agree on a literary term, I prefer using the term X Literature. The "X" represents the fact that most writers are members of Generation X and/or write about Gen X characters. In addition, the "X" represents the fact that it is a genre that defies exact literary classification, just as the generation defies exact designation. This may signify that we are entering a literary post-naming era, a "line's end end," as David Foster Wallace suggests.

X literature, in the fin de siècle [end of the century] tradition (in this case fin de millennium) is a composite of various literary and cultural forms. Aside from American modernism and postmodernism, X literature owes a great deal to the American Beats and the New or postmodern journalists. In addition, X literature is reminiscent of such late 19th Century/ early 20th Century American realists as Stephen Crane, Frank Norris, and Theodore Drieser whose novels were written in a documentary style and depicted the objective reality of "average" people and their everyday engagement with the environment. However, we have moved into a postmodern era, where American culture itself has become increasingly surreal. Therefore any "realistic" fiction must be a reflection of the surreality in contemporary society brought about primarily by the pervasive spread of popular culture. Above all other influences, X literature is most heavily dependent on popular culture (i.e., television, movies, and music), which have become "texts" of equal influence in the contemporary postmodern world.

Many literary reviewers have criticized young American writers for a preoccupation with popular culture that denigrates their fiction into intellectually flimsy material. There is a contradiction in this claim. The so-called "flat and affectless" tone of many works of X literature is actually similar to that achieved in the minimalist writings of Ernest Hemingway. Most critics are aware that Hemingway purposely chose to write in a less revealing dialogue-driven style. The best writing, as Hemingway claimed, showed only the tip of the iceberg. However, most literary critics are not willing to acknowledge that there is a similar submerged, hidden meaning to the works of X writers. X writers tend to write colloquial dialogue-driven fiction that abounds in popular culture references, but they do so in a manner that is both a realistic and penetrating form of social commentary. X writer David Foster Wallace believes the shift in the style of contemporary narrative is largely due to the influence of television in contemporary American society. In his essay, "E Unibus Pluram: Television and U.S. Fiction," Wallace defends his fellow young writers:

> Television has formed and trained us. It won't do then, for the literary establishment simply to complain that, for instance, young-written characters don't have very interesting dialogues with each other. That may be, but the truth is that in younger Americans' experience, people in the same room don't do all that much direct conversing with each other. What most people I know do is they all sit and face the same direction and stare at the same thing and then structure commercial-length conversations around the sorts of questions myopic car-crash witnesses might ask each other. Did you just see what I just saw? . . .

X literature is a product of America's MTV/Nuclear Age of the 1980's and of the contemporary 1990's Information/Electronic Age. Fredric Jameson has argued that postmodernism has arisen out of late capitalism and the globalization of the world market after the Second World War. But by the mid- to late-1980's and certainly by the 1990's, there has been a revelation of the social and individual effects of a global, rampant capitalism based on consumerism. The 1980's ushered in a new phase of American capitalism which involved the cultural domination of an "individual," whose "identity" became largely determined by consumer/popular/postmodern culture. In 1980's and 1990's America, mass media and popular culture have merged to become epistemologically dominating. As Stephen Connor argues in *Postmodern Culture*, "The new era of communication invades our minds in a pornographic way, ejecting all interiority, injecting the exterior world of television and information." Most American Gen Xers grew up in this society: a fragmented remote-control culture of quick soundbites, and radio and television jingles.

Because of this, X literature demands a prerequisite familiarity with popular culture and media in order to be fully understood. Effectively, a symbiosis has been forged between popular culture and identity in contemporary postmodern America. As Larry McCaffery argues, there has been "a prodigious expansion of culture throughout the social realm, to the point at which everything in our social life—from economic value and state power practice to the very structure of the psyche—can be said to have become cultural in some original and yet untheorized sense." Popular culture has become the primary text of reference for X writers. Whereas John Barth claimed in his postmodern treatise "The Literature of Replenishment" that a true postmodern writer has "a foot in the narrative past," most X writers have both feet firmly planted in the cultural past. Popular culture allied with mass media have set up a rival history of their own, complete with modernistic and postmodernistic forms. X writers typically rely on popular cultural history rather than narrative or literary history as substance for their works.

How X Literature Departs from Postmodernism

Canonized postmodern writers tend to revel in postmodern (dis)integration as literarily and culturally liberating, but to most X writers, postmodern (dis)integration has the serious potential to become a personally destructive form of empty decadence. In X literature, popular culture is often portrayed as a prison of postmodern fragmentary thought. It has resulted in the production of either manipulated, emotionally impoverished persons or cognizant disgruntled consumers, who recognize their emotional and psychic isolation in a dissolute consumer-based postmodern culture (often called "Slackers" in X literature or films for their attempt to live economically unfettered by America's consumer/corporate system). Most X novels reveal either one group or the other to the reader, while habitually exposing a hidden or overt sense of emotional damage, despondency, or vacuity. Most X novels implicitly argue that corporate society, dominated by the elder Silent or Baby Boomer generation, has created a fragmented postmodern culture under the illusory guise of being a "Global Village," linked together by mass media and popular culture. X writers have somewhat of a schizophrenic attitude towards popular/postmodern culture. While they often regard it as hyper-real, dissolute, and personally damaging, they have a sentimental relationship with postmodern/popular culture which has virtually defined their identities. Typically, Gen Xers describe this attitude as "irony," a contradictory love/hate relationship with their culture and themselves. Consequently, some X writers try to either manufacture a new culture (the term "alternative" in music and "independent" in films signifies the Gen X desire for artistic autonomy) for themselves or escape culture entirely.

In the tradition of the American realists and modernists, most X writers return the individual as the focus of the narrative, but the individual is one who contains multitudes (more multitudes that Walt Whitman could have ever imagined!), or one who has become a veritable microcosm of popular culture. Effectively, the "individual" is nullified and becomes a subject or a simulacrum, basing his or her behavior on the mass-media simulacrum of the real. In some X fiction, the characters go through a postmodern existential crisis in which they realize their essential meaninglessness or emptiness as popular culture simulacrums in a postmodern society already adrift in such forms. Other characters continue in their image-based existence—they simply "Deal with it," as one of Bret Easton Ellis' characters, Sean Bateman, frequently repeats in *The Rules of Attraction* (1987). In either case, most X writers or characters attempt to use literature and narrative to construct a virtual map of the postmodern cultural world. They endeavor to give an unfragmented shape or structure to their often jumbled postmodern psyches and disjointed personal experiences, while questioning contemporary cultural progress.

CHAPTER 3

Postmodern Writers and Their Works

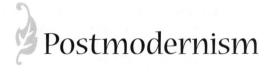

Postmodernism

Catch-22:
Postmodernism Looks
at World War II

Walter James Miller

Walter James Miller, professor emeritus of English at
New York University, has written extensively on a
number of American writers considered to be important early postmodernists. Among those writers he
has studied are Kurt Vonnegut Jr. and Joseph Heller,
whose 1961 novel *Catch-22* is the subject of this excerpt. Miller examines several aspects of this
groundbreaking novel, which helped change the way
in which writers treated the subject of World War II
and war in general. Miller focuses on the satirical
aspects of the book, analyzing the ways in which
Heller distorts and parodies the language and behavior of the military and its industrial partners to make
his point. He also notes the significant impact that
Catch-22 has had on the later success of other
prominent postmodernists.

Consider a novel that has been described like this. It is fat,
overlong, experimental in structure, intricate in texture. It
abounds in allusions, symbols, allegory. It's surrealistic,
Dadaist, absurdist, Dantean. Its message is savagely radical:
it satirizes cherished notions from the value of the family to
the viability of God.

Offhand you would say it sounds like an avant-garde work
doomed to be admired—perhaps exegesed—by a small following. You would be unprepared to hear these additional
facts. *Catch-22*, as it's called, enjoys worldwide popularity. Its
author, Joseph Heller, is the greatest-selling writer of serious
fiction in American history. Since *Catch-22* appeared in 1961,
it has helped create such a demand for innovative fiction that
America-at-large suddenly recognized another experimental

Excerpted from "Joseph Heller's Fiction," by Walter James Miller, in *American Writing
Today*, edited by Richard Kostelanetz (Troy, NY: Whitson Publishing Co., 1991). Copyright © 1991 by Richard Kostelanetz. Reprinted with permission from the author.

writer of Heller's own generation—the long-neglected Kurt Vonnegut—and made best-sellers too out of younger innovators like Thomas Pynchon, E.L. Doctorow, and Robert Coover. Many anomalies for which *Catch-22* prepared the public include this: Heller's second and third novels—*Something Happened* (1974) and *Good as Gold* (1979)—differ so radically from the first, they could have been written by two other innovators.

How could Heller perform such a miracle: producing avant-garde art that appeals to a mass audience? He got history and humor to work hand in hand. In the 1960s many Americans were beginning to question the morality of Uncle Sam's military ventures in Southeast Asia. Increasingly they were doubting the wisdom, even the motives, of many business, professional, and governmental leaders. As the number of citizens suspecting that a rationalist society might be irrational grew and grew, so did the sales of *Catch-22*. Seemingly an attack on the military-industrial complex of World War II, in which Heller had flown 60 combat missions, the novel actually aims, through highly original use of anachronisms, to expose the entire power system of the postwar world. Heller even foresaw many of the emerging crises of our times. *Catch-22* provides not only a catchphrase to describe modern frustrations, but also Scripture, complete with prophecy and identification of Satan, for the new counterculture.

But Heller's sense of timing would have availed him little, given the unorthodoxy of his approach, if he had not seduced his reader with black humor and absurdist wit. Step by step the reader braving Heller's strange terrain is rewarded with irreverent gags that promise shocking revelations. "Nately had a bad start. He came from a good family." "All over the world, young men were dying for what they had been told was their country.". . .

THE CENTRAL THEMES OF *CATCH-22*

Ostensibly, the story focuses on the exploits of the 256th Squadron, operating from the Mediterranean isle of Pianosa to bomb the Nazis' Gothic Line in Italy and installations in France. Yossarian, the main character in a cast of 60 well-defined individuals, earns a captaincy and a medal because he dared a second run over a well-armed, now fully alerted, target. But whenever he nears the number of missions he must fly to earn a tour of non-combat duty, his ambitious superiors keep raising that number far beyond the official Army requirement. They want to build up the best record of any unit. That's easier with seasoned veterans like Nately and Yossarian than with the green recruits who would replace them. Likely to die not for his country but for his colonels, finding all avenues of appeal blocked by those same commanders, Yossarian tries to escape the trap by feigning illness, even insanity. Obviously a crazy airman must be grounded. But there's a catch. He must ask to be grounded, and anyone asking to be excused from combat duty thereby proves he's not crazy. He "would be crazy to fly more missions and sane if he didn't, but if he was sane he had to fly them. If he flew them he was crazy and didn't have to; but if he didn't want to he was sane and had to." *Catch-22* becomes the master symbol, its many variations representing loopholes in the law that mean the powerful can take away the rights of their fellow citizens. Realizing that the Establishment itself has become Evil Incarnate, Yossarian deserts, following a long line of American dropouts, real and fictional, who decide to obey the Higher Conscience: Henry David Thoreau, hero of his autobiographical *Civil Disobedience*, Mark Twain's Huckleberry Finn, Ernest Hemingway's Lieutenant Henry.

Actually, Heller crams into 1944–1945 telling samples of American history from the crowding of the Indians off their own land in the 1800s to the controversies rampant in the Eisenhower Administration (1953–1961). Flashbacks were old tools when Heller used them to uncover corruption in, for example, the medical profession; what was new was his technique of creating fictional events in one period of time (World War II) that parodied actual events that would not occur until a later period (the 1950s). Senator Joseph McCarthy's 1954 anti-Communist battle cry, "Who promoted Major Peress?" is analyzed as an absurd question, "Who promoted Major Major?" Because his first name is Major, an IBM machine reads that as his rank. Heller's answer to McCarthy is typically symbolic. No one is guilty of promoting the Communist Peress; a machine, an organization operating automatically, did it. And the implications of Secretary of Defense Charles Wilson's blooper, "What's good for General Motors is good for the country and vice versa," are dramatized as Lieutenant Milo Minderbinder's black-market policy: "What's good for M&M Enterprises is good for the country."

Black-market tactics become Heller's symbol for free enterprise itself; it upholds the consumer's freedom to pay high
prices or starve. Some of Heller's anachronisms involve such
accurate extrapolations, from conditions rampant when he
was writing, that they prepared readers for life in the 1960s
and 1970s: like scandals in the U.S. agricultural programs
and in the Vietnam war.

HELLER'S UNORTHODOX APPROACH TO STORYTELLING

Heller's overall time-structure was one of his technical experiments making humor necessary as an inducement.
Soon after Yossarian sees, or thinks, of someone or something, he/Heller shies away from this experience, spiraling
back over previous action, spiraling so that all events
past-present-future are revealed in simultaneity. This recy-
cling continues so long as Yossarian is at the mercy of the
"spinning reasonableness" of *Catch-22.* But as soon as he
takes definite steps to break out of the vicious cycle, the action becomes linear. Thus the novel's "story-line" resembles
the path of a homing aircraft that circles an airport several
times before it gets "on the beam" and flies straight in.

Shying, spiraling in the first 38 chapters determines the
way, for example, Yossarian's most traumatic experience is
revealed to us. Eight times he recalls the dying of Snowden,
a gunner wounded over Avignon. Each time we get further
details before Yossarian shies. Not until he is close to resolv-
ing his problem can he bear, in Chapter 41, to recall the entire scene. Some early readers, even some critics, missed the
psychological validity behind this kind of narration. They
saw instead only repetition and thought Heller inept.

Psychological reality also guides Heller when he has
characters "feel" their way through crises not by thinking in
words but by reliving, or reflecting on, archetypal situations.
After Yossarian sabotages a mission, he copes with guilt feel-
ings. Walking across the isle, he sees a soldier eating a
pomegranate. This reminds the reader of Persephone, who
lost her innocence by tasting pomegranate in Hades. Yossarian enters a forest, itself a classical symbol of descent into
the shadow side of existence. In sudden darkness he's fright-
ened by burgeoning mushrooms. We know by now that for
an airman, they suggest exploding flak and so, especially
since they spring here out of black Hades, death itself. Limp
and pale, they suggest impotence, dread reward for him anx-

ious over guilt. But Yossarian flees out onto the beach, a margin between two worlds, and enters the Mediterranean. In a ritual of baptism he swims until he feels clean. The scene especially signifies when we realize that Yossarian has been identified earlier, through allusions, with the protagonist of T. S. Eliot's *The Waste Land:* until now, Yossarian has feared death by water, that is, rebirth through baptism. Neither Yossarian nor the reader need verbalize these experiences as I have verbalized them here; the same symbols that work subliminally for the character work for the reader to reflect change of mood from anxiety to peace.

Yossarian "thinks" his way through another crisis while sitting naked in a tree, where Milo visits him. Through a combination of Yossarian's remarks, our own associations, and the chaplain's reflections on this tableau, we see Yossarian as Jesus on the cross and Adam at the tree, Milo the businessman as Satan.

WORDPLAY AND OTHER DISTORTIONS IN *CATCH-22*

Even characters whom we know only from the outside develop in terms of allusion and allegory. Since Major de Coverley's first name is never pronounced, we suspect he represents divinity; in some religions God's name is unutterable. But inevitably we think of a famous prude in English literature, Sir Roger de Coverley, and we find the name apt for the major. "Roger" is an Air Force code word for "Received and understood." To "roger" a woman means, in British slang, to have one's will of her; this resonates with ironies in Heller's overall situation.

Alerted that Heller characterizes through tag-names, we quickly grasp the nature of Nately (natally, suggesting newly-born, innocent, conscious of genealogy), of Luciana (who brings light into Yossarian's room), of Wintergreen (survival is his talent). Alerted that Heller describes through cultural allusions, we understand characters like Milo and Dobbs all the better if we recognize certain lines about them as parodies of Eliot, Whitman, Tennyson, Shakespeare.

Heller achieves his most memorable effects through surrealistic or expressionistic distortion. Since Milo's black-market operations are international in scope, they inevitably ally him with his counterparts in the Nazi war machine. These dealings take priority over declared national policies; as part of his "contracts" with the Germans, Milo bombs his own squadron. A congressional investigation clears him once he proves the transaction made a tidy profit for free enterprise. Heller thus dramatizes what he sees as the truth behind international cartels. They make a mockery of patriotism; they aid the enemy; businessmen may use the chaos of war to increase their power over (to fight) their own people. Heller's hospital scenes include a man so completely bandaged that no one has ever seen, heard, or touched the person inside. He seems to represent the *thing* that war reduces a man to. Or is the Soldier in White some sinister listening apparatus? Heller intensifies the nightmare quality of surreal situations by alternating them with realistic narration. For sheer descriptive power, metaphoric intensity, and poetic cadences, his realistic battle scenes are unsurpassed in the literature of war.

Catch-22, then, shows the individual in the clutches of monolithic organizations like armies, cartels, governments. Heller's next two novels deal with variations on the same theme. But they differ in that Heller gives greater attention to family relations as intermediate between the individual and his organization, and he popularizes other avant-garde techniques that suit his new situations.

The Crying of Lot 49: How *Not* to Resolve a Mystery

Phillip Brian Harper

Thomas Pynchon's 1966 novel *The Crying of Lot 49*
resides on almost every list of influential postmodernist books. Phillip Brian Harper, professor of English and American studies at New York University,
discusses the novel in terms of two main themes, entropy and uncertainty. The explicit presence of these
two themes in the novel represents for Harper the author's effort at creating a fictional work that wholly
embodies a postmodern mindset, right down to its
construction and narration. Harper draws on the
work of a number of other critics to demonstrate how
Pynchon constantly frustrates the reader's desire for
resolution in the novel, a technique that has become
almost synonymous with postmodernism since.

The plot of *The Crying of Lot 49* is widely familiar. The protagonist, Oedipa Maas, is a young California housewife who
is jarred out of her suburban existence when she becomes
the executor of the estate of her late lover, the wealthy devel-
oper Pierce Inverarity. In order to undertake her duty with respect to Inverarity's will, she leaves her home in Kinneret-
Among-the-Pines for the more southerly locale of San
Narciso, where Inverarity had been based. Once she does
this, she has a series of "revelations" that indicate to her the
existence of—and Pierce's involvement in—an underground
society known as the Tristero that communicates through an
illicit postal system called W.A.S.T.E., whose mailboxes mas-
querade as garbage cans. Two initial clues key her in to the
existence of the Tristero: One is a letter to her in San Narciso
from her husband, Mucho, on the envelope of which appears
the printed message, ostensibly from the post office, "RE-

Excerpted from *Framing the Margins: The Social Logic of Postmodern Culture*, by
Phillip Brian Harper. Copyright © 1994 by Phillip Brian Harper. Reprinted with permission from Oxford University Press, Inc.

PORT ALL OBSCENE MAIL TO YOUR POTSMASTER" (the subtle subversion of official postal slogans turns out to be a signal activity of the Tristero); the other is a symbol she discovers on the wall of the women's restroom in a San Narciso bar called The Scope, which she later figures to be a drawing of a bugle-like post horn with a mute in its bell. As she tries to untangle the intricacies of Pierce Inverarity's holdings, the clues proliferate—everywhere she sees the muted post horn, the initials W.A.S.T.E., references to Tristero or Trystero, until finally she learns that the very stamp collection over which Pierce had obsessed while he was alive is itself a relic of Tristero and the W.A.S.T.E. postal system. Unsure at last whether there really is a Tristero underground or she is only imagining it, whether the whole thing is a hoax perpetrated by Inverarity or she is insanely paranoid, Oedipa hopes to discover the truth by attending the auction at which the stamp collection is going to be sold off, where she waits to see who will bid on lot 49, which it constitutes. The novel ends on this note of anticipation, the only certainty being that the legacy Pierce Inverarity has left is coextensive with the intricacies of America itself, the secret of which Oedipa has actually, inadvertently, been seeking all along.

ENTROPY AS THE CENTRAL THEME OF THE NOVEL

As at least one critic has suggested, it is evident that "the plotline of *The Crying of Lot 49* follows that of the detective story, wherein a heroine-sleuth attempts to solve a mystery through the logical assembling and interpretation of palpable evidence." It is also true, as Lance Olsen further points out, that *Lot 49* "reverses" that conventional plotline: "The movement becomes one from certainty to uncertainty." As Stefano Tani puts it, *Lot 49* "'deconstructs' conventional detective fiction," as it presents "a structural non-solution . . . a proliferation of clues which lead nowhere." This situation of epistemological uncertainty holds true both for the reader—as Frank Palmeri notes, the novel "raises expectations of meaning that it satisfies partially or not at all"—and for Oedipa herself—Olsen observes that "[a]lthough for Oedipa meaning always seems near . . . [,] it never materializes." Indeed, at one point during her quest, Oedipa herself wonders whether "at the end of this . . . , she . . . might not be left with only compiled memories of clues, announcements, intimations, but never the central truth itself"; later, she considers whether "the gemlike 'clues' were only some kind of compensation. To make up for her having lost the direct, epileptic Word. . . ."

If the uncertainty that characterizes *The Crying of Lot 49* substantiates Lance Olsen's claim that Pynchon "revels in ultimate confusion and indeterminacy," it is also true that it is based in a very specific theoretical notion about the nature of indeterminacy. Ever since the appearance of Anne Mangel's founding article on the subject in 1971, critics have discussed the import for *The Crying of Lot 49* of the concept of entropy—a concept that has dual significance in the fields of thermodynamics and information theory. Deriving his formulation from a standard dictionary entry, Peter L. Abernethy actually offers the most concise explanation of the meaning of entropy in those two fields:

> Thermodynamics defines entropy as "the degradation of the matter and energy in the universe to an ultimate state of inert uniformity." In communications it is "a measure of the amount of information in a message that is based on the logarithm of the number of possible equivalent messages" (i.e., the more ambiguous the message, the more entropic it is).

Robert Newman further specifies the significance of entropy in its different contexts: Because "[i]n thermodynamic theory entropy refers to . . . a uniform randomness that allows for no differentiation among the parts of a system . . . [,] maximum entropy yields a chaos of sameness." On the other hand, "[i]n information theory . . . disorganization increases the potential information that may be conveyed. Maximum entropy in this respect produces a chaos of multiplicity."

IMPLICATING THE READER

Overlaid onto social and cultural contexts, these two notions of entropy provide a workable metaphor for the development in the plot of Pynchon's novel. As Newman points out, "[a]t the beginning of the novel Oedipa's conventionality and the lifeless repetition the reader encounters in the traces of American culture suggest an entropic system in the thermodynamic sense." And, indeed, such a system is indicated in Pynchon's description of Oedipa's life up until she is named executor of Inverarity's estate—"a fat deckful of days which seemed (wouldn't she be first to admit it?) more or less identical," or in the appearance of San Narciso as Oedipa first approaches it in her car:

> Like many named places in California it was less an identifi-
> able city than a grouping of concepts—census tracts, special
> purpose bond-issue districts, shopping nuclei, all overlaid
> with access roads to its own freeway. . . . if there was any vi-
> tal difference between it and the rest of Southern California,
> it was invisible on first glance.

As Newman further suggests, however, as the novel pro-
gresses Oedipa seems to enter into a system that is entropic
in informational terms, since "the estate that Inverarity
leaves Oedipa to sort out yields more and more information
about that system . . . , to the point that its diversity becomes
bewildering," hence the unresolved nature of Oedipa's quest
at the end of the novel. The defining characteristic of *The
Crying of Lot 49* (as with all of Pynchon's novels), however,
is the degree to which not only the characters but the readers themselves are implicated in the uncertainty that the
story manifests. As John Leland puts it,

> Pynchon's novel is not only about entropy but is itself
> entropic. . . .
>   The entropic nature of communication informs both
> Oedipa's quest to sort out the earthly effects of Inverarity and
> our attempts to sort out the "results" of Oedipa's experience—
> that is, to sort out the information Pynchon provides about his
> novel.

Moreover, the uncertainty that we and Oedipa experience as
Pynchon's plot unfolds is also thematized rhetorically in the
narrative. It is a critical commonplace to say that Pynchon's
syntactic structures in *The Crying of Lot 49* foster a profound
semantic multiplicity; what remains is to identify the specific ramifications of that multiplicity. A look at one of Pynchon's characteristic narrative techniques will shed some
light on the exact import of his postmodernist strategy.

THE UNCERTAIN NARRATOR

Richard Pearce has claimed that in *The Crying of Lot 49*,
Pynchon "abandons the stable omniscient perspective to focus on Oedipa Maas's developing consciousness; the narrator only knows what Oedipa knows at each step in her
quest." While it is true that the narrator of *Lot 49* is not at all
omniscient in the standard manner, the imperfectness of his
knowledge, which approximates Oedipa's own uncertainty,
is much more disorienting than the latter. Relatively early in
the book, we already can spot passages by which we can dis-
cern the non-omniscience of the narrator. In chapter 2,

Oedipa, just arrived in San Narciso, is sharing wine and tequila with Metzger, the lawyer who drew up Pierce Inverarity's will, while the TV plays an old movie in which Metzger starred as the child actor Baby Igor. As they get increasingly tipsy, Metzger challenges Oedipa to place a bet on the outcome of the movie. Finally, she relents: "'So,' she yelled, maybe a bit rattled, 'I bet a bottle of something. Tequila, all right? . . .'" Right after this, having realized by his response that Metzger is interested not in more alcohol but in sex, Oedipa "grew more and more angry, perhaps juiced, perhaps only impatient for the movie to come back on." At another point in the novel, the narrator relates for us Oedipa's discovery of the "potsmaster" slogan on her letter from Mucho, and attempts to correlate it with her discovery of the post horn logo, noting that "[i]t may have been that same evening that they happened across The Scope," the bar in which Oedipa first sights the emblem. Finally, once Oedipa is fully embroiled in her quest for the meaning of the Tristero, she spends a delirious evening tracking clues throughout San Narciso, fighting sleep as she goes. As the narrator puts it, "What fragments of dreams came [to her] had to do with the post horn. Later, possibly, she would have trouble sorting the night into real and dreamed."

MERGING DISCOURSES

A common characteristic of all of these passages is their use of adverbs of uncertainty—"maybe," "perhaps," "possibly"—adverbs that indicate the narrator's lack of sureness about the events being described. To a large degree, that lack of sureness can, as Richard Pearce claims, be read as a sign of the congruence of the narrator's knowledge with that of Oedipa. After all, the style of the passages in question can be identified as a form of "free indirect discourse," which is characterized by Tzvetan Todorov as

> a discourse that presents itself at first glance as an indirect style (that is, it includes marks of time and person corresponding to a discourse on the part of the author) but is penetrated, in its syntactic and semantic structure, by enunciative properties, thus by the discourse of the character.

It is as an element in Oedipa's discourse, then, that we can identify the uncertainty in the passages under consideration: If Oedipa is presented as "*maybe* a bit rattled" when she wagers a bottle of tequila with Metzger, this could be

because the passage in question represents her own uncertain reflection on her state of mind at the time of the bet
rather than an indirect assessment by the novel's narrator;
the same situation obtains in the description of Oedipa as
"perhaps juiced, *perhaps* only impatient . . ."; the speculation
that the night on which Oedipa first noticed the "potsmaster"
reference "may have been" the same evening on which she
discovered the post horn logo at The Scope can similarly be
read as Oedipa's own attempt, after the fact, to settle the sequence of events in her mind; and, if we follow the logic of
the preceding example, then the narrative reflection that
"[l]ater, possibly, she would have trouble sorting the night
into real and dreamed" would represent Oedipa's anticipatory musing about her psychic state in the future, after the
disorienting night is over.

But there is not a true parallel between this "anticipatory"
passage and the "retrospective" one that precedes it in my
discussion. While it is true that all four of the passages under
consideration are "penetrated . . . by the discourse of the
character," Oedipa, even as they are presented as specifically
narrative discourse, their significance as instances of free indirect style varies depending on the tense that characterizes
them. The first two passages that I cite occur in the context
of a simple-past-tense narrative, conventional in realist fictional discourse, with the effect that the cognition of the narrator seems merged in that of Oedipa at the moment that the
described events are taking place. The perfect-past-tense
construction of the third example functions similarly, with
the narrator's cognition apparently subsumed in Oedipa's as
she engages in a relatively realistic retrospection about her
first evening at The Scope. The fourth, anticipatory passage,
however, jars in the context of the pattern I have noted. It
does this not because it is impossible to see the narrator's
cognitive capacity absorbed in Oedipa's as she anticipates
what her memory of her peripatetic night will be; rather, it
jars precisely because that absorption itself paradoxically reminds us of the radical distinction between narrator and
character that normally obtains in conventional fictional discourse. Because it seems feasible to us that a character might
be represented as unsure of her own state of mind at any
given juncture, or as uncertain about the exact sequence of a
set of events that happened in the past, then it is easy for us
to read the first three passages I have cited as relatively con-

ventional instances of free indirect discourse as I have described it above, with the narrator's customary omniscience yielding to the less reliable knowledge of the character for the sake of a particular realistic narrative effect. That effect—the sense of a character's cognitive fallibility—can only be achieved, however, in a narrative context in which the character might realistically be presented as effectively knowing in the first place. That condition does not obtain in the case of the anticipatory passage I have cited, since there is no way a character might realistically be presented as knowledgeable about what her state of mind will be at any given point in the future. The passage under consideration is unusual, then, not simply because, read as an instance of free indirect discourse, it presents the narrator as deferring to a character's imperfect knowledge about a given realm but because the realm in question—the fictional future engaged by the novel—is precisely the one regarding which the traditional narrator's omniscience is usually made manifest. Indeed, we might say that narrative itself depends upon a narrator's knowledge of what will happen next. Consequently, the uncertainty in the statement that "later, possibly, [Oedipa] would have trouble sorting the night into real and dreamed" jars us because it is posited in the context of a future about which we would never expect a character to have reliable knowledge anyway, and, further, because it represents the failure of the text to buttress the character's limited knowledge through recourse to the narratorial omniscience that conventionally governs the representation of the fictional future. Thus the uncertainty in this passage is much more unsettling than that in the more conventional instances of free indirect discourse, since rather than representing merely the subsumption of the narrator's cognition in that of the character, this passage represents the apparent *failure* of the narrator's cognitive ability in such a way that the whole ontology of the fictive world—which is conventionally expressed through, if not created by, the narrator—is rendered apparently unstable. The disorienting nature of Pynchon's novel, then, derives not merely from the subjective uncertainty represented in the single character of Oedipa but rather from the fact that indeterminacy appears to be an objective phenomenon that characterizes the whole world of the novel—a universal effect not traceable to the specific circumstances in which individual characters find themselves.

THE IMPERFECT NARRATOR AND THE POSTMODERN WORLD

This is the effect that obtains, at any rate, if we consider the narrator's uncertainty in light of his relation to the fictive world that we take him to be shaping for us, as readers conditioned to suspend reasonable disbelief in order to accept the "realistic" quality of a conventional work of fiction. For, in relation to that world, the conventional third-person narrator—as the fictive stand-in for the author, however disparate those two personae might otherwise be—assumes the status of a primary ordering force that endows phenomena with their objective significance. Thus, the discovery of the narrator's imperfection suggests a similar and analogous lack of coherency in the organization of the "real" world that we inhabit, a lack of objective meaning in life that, while disorienting, is nonetheless familiar and recognizable, insofar as it constitutes the signal crisis of the modern age.

If, on the other hand, we consider the implications of narratorial uncertainty in light of the relation between the narrator and *ourselves,* the readers, then we might be inclined to take the matter much more personally and, thus, to find its implications rather more startling. For, in relation to the *reader,* as opposed to the world of the novel, the narrator represents not so much an objective organizational force as a mirror for our own subjective efforts to construct effective systems of meaning. From *this* perspective, then, the discovery of the narrator's imperfection suggests a similar and analogous lack of coherency in our own psychic subjectivity, and thus the introjection of the modern crisis of meaning into the human subject itself with the consequent emergence of a crisis of self-cognition that is specifically *post*modern.

Slaughterhouse-Five: Restructuring Time and Space

Jerome Klinkowitz

Jerome Klinkowitz is a professor of English at the University of Northern Iowa in Cedar Falls. He has been an especially important figure in gaining academic acceptance for a number of writers of postmodern fiction, perhaps most notably, Kurt Vonnegut Jr. In this piece, Klinkowitz discusses a number of ways in which Vonnegut's 1969 novel *Slaughterhouse-Five* can be described as postmodern. In particular, Klinkowitz focuses on the ways in which the decidedly postmodern structure of the novel reflects Vonnegut's personal effort to overcome his traumatic experiences as an unintentional victim of the firebombing of the German city of Dresden in World War II. Klinkowitz argues that Vonnegut intentionally distorts traditional ideas of time and space in the novel as a representation of the psychological destruction suffered by those who personally witnessed the horrors of mass destruction such as that in Dresden. The unusual form of the novel, Klinkowitz maintains, is the result of Vonnegut's attempt to make a new and better meaning for the world—since he argues that the old one inevitably resulted in destruction and lies—through the use of his imagination.

Slaughterhouse-Five is a triumph of Vonnegut's imagination, a product of twenty years of prototypes where at last the author has found a way to emphasize benign constructions of the world, and forget about the bad. The firebombing of Dresden was, throughout Vonnegut's career, never far beneath the surface. With his growing prominence he became explicit, adding to a 1966 reissue of *Mother Night* a revealing introduction, detailing the extent of his own "personal experience with Nazi monkey business." Two years in residence at the University of Iowa Writers Workshop gave him the financial support and free mornings to complete his "Dresden book." The firebombing itself would prove to be his block: in one draft Vonnegut envisioned the typography becoming darker and darker, running together as the date of the bombing—February 13, 1945—drew near, until at that narrative point the pages would be entirely black, then slowly clearing away into legibility as the event receded into history. What Vonnegut did send to his publisher (and to *Ramparts* magazine, who politely inquired if this was all there was to the manuscript) was a strange, apparently disjointed account, beginning with Vonnegut himself and ranging on to include the lifetime adventures of one Billy Pilgrim, "a novel somewhat in the telegraphic schizophrenic manner of tales of the planet Tralfamadore, where the flying saucers come from." In the first chapter Vonnegut spoke directly to his publisher and editor, Seymour Lawrence. "It is so short and jumbled and jangled, Sam, because there is nothing intelligent to say about a massacre."

ARTICULATING THE UNSPEAKABLE

Slaughterhouse-Five is a book about many difficult things to say. Billy Pilgrim faces death in Dresden and is asked to articulate it. He is also at the bedside of his dying mother; "'How did I get so *old?*'" is her unanswerable question. But Vonnegut, with his customary hilarity in the face of the unspeakable, offers a parable for Billy's aphasia. He's drunk, trying to start his car and drive home after a party:

> The main thing now was to find the steering wheel. First, Billy windmilled his arms, hoping to find it by luck. When that didn't work, he became methodical, working in such a way that the wheel could not possibly escape him. He placed himself hard against the left-hand door, searched every square inch of the area before him. When he failed to find the wheel, he moved over six inches and searched again. Amazingly, he was eventually hard against the right-hand door, without having found the wheel. He concluded that somebody had stolen it. This angered him as he passed out.

What the eminently logical Billy doesn't know is that "He was in the back seat of his car, which was why he couldn't find the steering wheel."

Vonnegut delights in such challenges to our smug knowledge "of what's *really* going on." In *Breakfast of Champions* (1973) he describes a work of science fiction, of sorts: "Kilgore Trout once wrote a short story which was a dialogue between two pieces of yeast. They were discussing the possible purposes of life as they ate sugar and suffocated in their own excrement. Because of their limited intelligence, they never came close to realizing that they were making champagne." Vonnegut's credo is never to be the victim of such short-sightedness himself. But the matter of Dresden presents a special problem. After a plane crash Billy is hospitalized with the official Air Force historian of World War II, who is revising his work into a single-volume edition. "The thing was, though, there was almost nothing in the [original] twenty-seven volumes about the Dresden raid, even though it had been such a howling success. The extent of the success had been kept a secret for many years after the war—a secret from the American people. It was no secret from the Germans, of course, or from the Russians, who occupied Dresden after the war, who are in Dresden still." To this Billy can only say, "I was there," and try to avoid the stylization and phoniness which characterize war stories, be they the Frank Sinatra-John Wayne heroics which Vonnegut's war buddy's wife Mary O'Hare detests, or the British prisoners who turn their captivity into *The Pirates of Penzance*. Either way is a hopelessly bad lie, especially for the otherwise admirable British—"They could tunnel all they pleased. They would inevitably surface within a rectangle of barbed wire, would find themselves greeted listlessly by dying Russians."

HOW *SLAUGHTERHOUSE-FIVE* QUESTIONS FREE WILL

Slaughterhouse-Five is most notable for bringing up the question of what surely is—according to Vonnegut—the greatest lie of all, dwarfing Dresden with its cosmic implications. "If I hadn't spent so much time studying Earthlings," remarks a Tralfamadorian to Billy Pilgrim, "I wouldn't have any idea of what was meant by 'free will.' I've visited thirty-one inhabited planets in the universe, and I have studied reports on one hundred more. Only on Earth is there any talk of free will." What possibilities there are for "better lies" beyond free will are considered by Vonnegut through his metaphor of "time travel," which serves both as a resolution of the story's theme and as a technique for expressing the truth of these facts within the structure of a novel. In his fifth chapter Vonnegut has described a Tralfamadorian novel, and the scheme is familiar of recent innovative works on our own planet, including those of [Richard] Brautigan, [Steve] Katz, [Donald] Barthelme, [Jerzy] Kosinski, [Robert] Coover, and Vonnegut himself:

> each clump of symbols is a brief, urgent message—describing a situation, a scene. We Tralfamadorians read them all at once, not one after the other. There isn't any particular relationship between all the messages, except that the author has chosen them carefully, so that, when seen all at once, they produce an image of life that is beautiful and surprising and

BILLY PILGRIM'S UNUSUAL LIFE

Billy Pilgrim, the protagonist of Slaughterhouse-Five, *is a character whose life-story includes a number of tragic events, most notably the firebombing of Dresden, Germany, at the end of World War II. For Billy, though, these events do not occur in strict chronological order. This excerpt shows how Vonnegut intentionally confuses this situation, presenting it either as a kind of science-fictional reality or the result of Billy's repeated psychological trauma.*

Listen:

Billy Pilgrim has come unstuck in time.

Billy has gone to sleep a senile widower and awakened on his wedding day. He has walked through a door in 1955 and come out another one in 1941. He has gone back through that door to find himself in 1963. He has seen his birth and death many times, he says, and pays random visits to all the events in between.

He says.

Billy is spastic in time, has no control over where he is going next, and the trips aren't necessarily fun. He is in a constant state of stage fright, he says, because he never knows what part of his life he is going to have to act in next.

Billy was born in 1922 in Ilium, New York, the only child of a barber there. He was a funny-looking child who became a funny-looking youth–tall and weak, and shaped like a bottle of Coca-Cola. He graduated from Ilium High School in the upper third of his class, and attended night sessions at the Ilium School of Optometry for one semester before being drafted for military service in the Second World War. His father died in a hunting accident during the war. So it goes.

deep. There is no beginning, no middle, no end, no moral, no causes, no effects. What we love in our books are the depths of many marvelous moments seen all at one time.

Such experiences are not at all unearthly; Billy practices spatial juxtapositions even when he is not time-traveling, as when a drive through the gutted Ilium ghetto reminds him of Dresden in ruins. Throughout the book (and in all his works) Vonnegut plays with such hop-scotching images: a radium watch dial in Mammoth Cave, a few pages later the faces of Russian prisoners described the same way, and so forth.

In previous novels Vonnegut reorganized human ethics, history, and theology; *Slaughterhouse-Five* presents his greatest restructuring, that of time and space. The Tralfama-

---

Billy saw service with the infantry in Europe, and was taken prisoner by the Germans. After his honorable discharge from the Army in 1945, Billy again enrolled in the Ilium School of Optometry. During his senior year there, he became engaged to the daughter of the founder and owner of the school, and then suffered a mild nervous collapse.

He was treated in a veteran's hospital near Lake Placid, and was given shock treatments and released. He married his fiancée, finished his education, and was set up in business in Ilium by his father-in-law. Ilium is a particularly good city for optometrists because the General Forge and Foundry Company is there. Every employee is required to own a pair of safety glasses, and to wear them in areas where manufacturing is going on. GF&F has sixty-eight thousand employees in Ilium. That calls for a lot of lenses and a lot of frames.

Frames are where the money is.

Billy became rich. He had two children, Barbara and Robert. In time, his daughter Barbara married another optometrist, and Billy set him up in business. Billy's son Robert had a lot of trouble in high school, but then he joined the famous Green Berets. He straightened out, became a fine young man, and he fought in Vietnam.

Early in 1968, a group of optometrists, with Billy among them, chartered an airplane to fly them from Ilium to an international convention of optometrists in Montreal. The plane crashed on top of Sugarbush Mountain, in Vermont. Everybody was killed but Billy. So it goes.

Kurt Vonnegut Jr., *Slaughterhouse-Five, or The Children's Crusade: A Duty Dance with Death.* New York: Seymour Lawrence/Delacorte, 1969, pp. 20–21.

dorians (Vonnegut's creation) have spatialized time, balancing a horizontal or linear determinism with a vertical, modal freedom. As Billy Pilgrim recounts:

> The most important thing I learned on Tralfamadore was that when a person dies he only *appears* to die. He is still very much alive in the past, so it is very silly for people to cry at his funeral. All moments, past, present, and future, always have existed, always will exist. The Tralfamadorians can look at all the different moments just the way we can look at a stretch of the Rocky Mountains, for instance. They can see how permanent all the moments are, and they can look at any moment that interests them. It's just an illusion we have here on Earth that one moment follows another one, like beads on a string, and that once a moment is gone it is gone forever.
>
> When a Tralfamadorian sees a corpse, all he thinks is that the dead person is in a bad condition in that particular moment, but that the same person is just fine in plenty of other moments. Now, when I myself hear that somebody is dead, I simply shrug and say what the Tralfamadorians say about dead people, which is 'So it goes.'

The justification for such restructuring is the bad experience Vonnegut's characters have had with life so far. Of Eliot Rosewater [the protagonist of *God Bless You, Mr. Rosewater* (1965)] and Billy Pilgrim, Vonnegut says, "They had both found life meaningless, partly because of what they had seen in the war. Rosewater, for instance, had shot a fourteen-year-old fireman, mistaking him for a German soldier. So it goes. And Billy had seen the greatest massacre in European history, which was the firebombing of Dresden. So it goes." Therefore "they were trying to re-invent themselves and their universe. Science fiction was a big help."

MAKING MEANING THROUGH IMAGINATION

To make it meaningful, the world must be reinvented. Science fiction time-travel is Vonnegut's metaphor, but behind this device stands man's greatest power, what separates him from other living creatures—the ability to imagine that anything, even he himself, is different from what is. Turn things around, make them different. Overcome the trouble, in one's mind to start with, but, when you have the technology, that way too. The horrors of war, our complex machines of destruction: why not reinvent them, as they would be reinvented when we take a war movie and run it backward:

> American planes, full of holes and wounded men and corpses, took off backwards from an airfield in England. Over

France, a few German fighter planes flew at them backwards, sucked bullets and shell fragments from some of the planes and crewmen. They did the same for wrecked American bombers on the ground, and those planes flew up backwards to join the formation.

The formation flew backwards over a German city that was in flames. The bombers opened their bomb bay doors, exerted a miraculous magnetism which shrunk the fires, gathered them into cylindrical steel containers, and lifted the containers into the bellies of the planes. The containers were stored neatly in racks. The Germans below had miraculous devices of their own, which were long steel tubes. They used them to suck more fragments from the crewmen and planes. But there were still a few wounded Americans, though, and some of the bombers were in bad repair. Over France, though, German fighters came up again, made everything and everybody as good as new.

When the bombers got back to their base, the steel cylinders were taken from the racks and shipped back to the United States of America, where factories were operating night and day, dismantling the cylinders, separating the dangerous contents into minerals. Touchingly, it was mainly women who did this work. The minerals were then shipped to specialists in remote areas. It was their business to put them into the ground, to hide them cleverly, so they would never hurt anybody ever again.

And so Vonnegut turns to a reconstruction of reality, to the human imagination, to art. In Chapter One of *Slaughterhouse-Five* he recalls his Guggenheim trip to Dresden and a book he took along, *Celine and His Vision* by Erika Ostrovsky. "Time obsessed him," Vonnegut noted of Celine. "Miss Ostrovsky reminded me of the amazing scene in *Death on the Installment Plan* where Celine wants to stop the bustling of a street crowd. He screams on paper, *Make them stop . . . don't let them move at all . . . There, make them freeze . . . once and for all! . . . So that they won't disappear any more!*"

Such radical use of the imagination to build a new freedom and dignity for man is part of Vonnegut's appeal to youth. In this respect his great following may seem to have run after a prophet, but there has been precious little guru-making of the man, certainly less than for [J.D.] Salinger and his Zen wisdom a decade ago, and nothing resembling the cult surrounding [J.R.R.] Tolkien. Rather, there is a great correspondence between what Vonnegut says when he appears at colleges, and what he wrote for the same students' parents in the days of the *Saturday Evening Post*. "We're not too young for love," a teenage runaway admits to her boyfriend in an early story. "Just too young for about everything else there is that goes with love." A decade later, in his Bennington commencement speech, Vonnegut was saying the same thing: that young people should not accept responsibility for reforming the world. In practical terms, that is an impossible duty for any human being to bear. The answer lies rather in our attitudes, our philosophies—in short, what comes from our imagination. Vonnegut's beliefs in human decency are perhaps the most consistent thing about his writing, whether it be the occasional stories in the *Post,* where basically good and simple people—storm window salesmen, small town businessmen—triumph over far more imposing people and ideas, or in the novels, where with much more artistic apparatus he sets about redefining our universe, which is, as he establishes, nothing more than a dominant state of mind.

Mumbo Jumbo and the Minority Perspective on Postmodern America

Erik D. Curren

Although postmodernism is a literary movement that has been accused (with some justification) of being a Eurocentric and white phenomenon, Ishmael Reed is an African-American author whose works can easily be placed within this category as well. Erik D. Curren, who received his Ph.D. in English from the University of California at Irvine, uses the theories of the French critic Jean-François Lyotard to define Reed's 1972 novel *Mumbo Jumbo* as postmodern. Curren claims that Reed's novel represents an example of what happens when a narrative culture and a scientific culture meet, a situation described at length by Lyotard in his important book, *The Postmodern Condition: A Report on Knowledge*. In this manner, Curren includes Reed retroactively among a group of writers often labeled postmodern who sought to bring art into a more social context.

For Ishmael Reed the history of Western culture is one of violence and domination. In his 1972 novel *Mumbo Jumbo*, Reed's unlikely spokesman for "high" art, police chief-turned-art-museum-curator Biff Musclewhite, explains with brutal candor the greatest threat to Western culture:

> Son, these niggers writing. Profaning our sacred words. Taking them from us and beating them on the anvil of BoogieWoogie, putting their black hands on them so that they shine like burnished amulets. Taking our words, son, these filthy niggers and using them like they were their god-given pussy. Why . . . why one of them dared to interpret, critically mind you, the great Herman Melville's *Moby-Dick!!*

Such a passage situates Reed's novel firmly amid the cul-

Excerpted from "Ishmael Reed's Postmodern Revolt," by Erik D. Curren, in *Literature and Film in the Historic Dimension*, edited by John D. Simons (Gainesville, FL: University Press of Florida). Copyright © 1994 by the Board of Regents of the State of Florida. Reprinted with the permission of the University Press of Florida.

tural politics of the Western world, politics that Reed engages through the formal devices of his postmodern text.

It has been said that while modernism maintains a strict distinction between literature and society, postmodernism denies any difference between aesthetic and other cultural production. What was really new about contemporary literature for critics of this phenomenon was its rejection of the idea of "high art" held by modernists like Marcel Proust, Thomas Mann, and James Joyce. Leslie Fiedler, for example, proposed in his seminal 1969 essay "Cross the Border—Close the Gap" that postmodernism had developed an anti-art aesthetic, a revised idea of the institution of art allowing for the use of elements of media and consumer culture, which permitted postmodernist works to represent the electronic fragmentation of contemporary life. Accordingly, contemporary art breaks out of the narrow confines of the prison house of bourgeois art and into society, closing the gap between high and popular art, and crossing the border separating the aesthetic from the practical world. . . .

What better place to look for a manifestation of the literary attempt to make art social than in minority literatures of the United States? It cannot be denied that works written by Americans of color are intimately involved with the political struggles for freedom and equality waged by many cultural groups. Since the Black Aesthetic movement, explicitly political and historical literature concerned with ethnic and racial oppression and the attempt to establish countercultural traditions has made a noticeable impact on the American literary and cultural scene. Writers like Toni Morrison, Maxine Hong Kingston, and Ishmael Reed have enjoyed considerable popularity due to a kind of postmodern literary pluralism.

If we focus on Reed we find the model of a politically committed writer. A novelist, poet and essayist, editor and publisher, Reed is above all a cultural critic who attempts to realize his vision of cultural pluralism both in his writings and in literary activism. This activism includes several projects to expand the canon of American literature and make it more useful to pluralist social praxis, ranging from the opening in 1976 of the Before Columbus Foundation—a producer and distributor of the works of little-known ethnic writers—to teaching at UC Berkeley, to lecturing around the country and contributing to publications in the U.S. and Europe. Not surprisingly, his fiction is committed to dealing with the historical situation of African-Americans and exploring the possibilities of their culture. From his first novel, *The Free-Lance Pallbearers* (1967)—the story of Bukka Doopeyduk, a would-be black revolutionary lynched after his abortive attempt to overthrow the totalitarian regime of Polish-American strongman Harry Sam—up to his most recent work, Reed's writing has tried to demystify the politics of race in the United States and beyond.

Mumbo Jumbo, Reed's best known novel, was written on the heel of the cultural upheaval of the late 1960s and deals with many of the cultural issues that had gained wide currency at the time. An avant-gardist work that goes beyond deconstructing realist conventions of coherence and readability to question the existence of art itself as an entity separate from society, *Mumbo Jumbo* tells a variety of stories in a disconnected narrative that resists all attempts to unify it. Alternately overlapping and parallel stories center on the encounter of two kinds of cultural organization in the history of the West: hierarchical order based on rationality, and egalitarianism founded on folk tradition. Reed focuses on a particular moment of this conflict, the United States of the 1920s, to construct his "main" plot, an allegory of the rise and fall of African-American culture associated with the Harlem Renaissance.

This flowering of black culture is represented by a psychic epidemic called "Jes Grew," named for the haphazard and undirected development of the black folk tradition from scattered cultural roots. The infection represents a threat to the straight-laced American cultural establishment because it causes people to eschew hard work for dancing, singing, and the celebration of bodily existence. Beginning in New Orleans, the cradle of American jazz culture, the epidemic spreads across the country toward New York, seeking what is cryptically referred to throughout the novel as "its text." On the way Jes Grew infects people of all racial, ethnic, and class groups, making them healthy by negating the control exercised over them by rationalism. About Jes Grew, the narrator tells us that "actually, it was an anti-plague. Some plagues caused the body to waste away; Jes Grew enlivened the host."

Despite its salutary effects, or rather because of them, the white rationalist mainstream—led by the Atonist Path, a conspiracy controlling all aspects of society and culture—

sees Jes Grew as a disease that threatens all social order. Reed notes that, "To some if you owned your own mind you were indeed sick but when you possessed an Atonist mind you were healthy." To put down the epidemic, the Atonist hierarchy mobilizes its "military arm," the "Wallflower Order" (standing for the Ivy League, as Gates notes), to direct the 1915 United States invasion of Haiti, aimed at the immediate source of Jes Grew, and to sanitize American culture. In an example of the kind of bold anachronism that powers much of Reed's humorous critique, the Wallflower Order in turn calls on the Knights Templar, known for their success in an earlier campaign of Western cultural imperialism, the medieval crusades. The scheming Grand Master of the Templars, Hinckle Von Vampton sets himself up as a patron of black arts in order to wage a disinformation campaign intended to dissipate the power of Jes Grew by turning its most likely carriers into black lumpenproletarians. Toward the end of manufacturing a false black consciousness friendly to the domination of white Western culture, Von Vampton publishes a literary rag sheet aimed at the black audience. This journal, aptly named *The Benign Monster*, features pornography and romantic depictions of street violence along with commentary demonstrating that black culture, when it gets beyond the usual primitive forms, is entirely derivative of the European High Art tradition.

Meanwhile Papa LaBas adept at African-inspired HooDoo, uses his arsenal of conjures to aid the spread of the "anti-plague" in hopes that it will liberate the whole country from the domination of rationalism and its repressive morality. From his Mumbo Jumbo Kathedral, LaBas, a man whom we are told carries Jes Grew inside him like other people carry DNA, uses a combination of HooDoo loas and Western science to challenge the power of Atonist alienated consciousness by getting people in touch with the pre-scientific side of their bodies and minds.

A MINIATURE HISTORY OF WESTERN CULTURE

The plot of Jes Grew is crossed by threads of connected subplots, which, taken together, create an account of Western cultural history from early Egypt through the 1920s and up to the civil rights movement of the sixties in a narrative that self-consciously mixes fiction and fact. Reed's book attempts simultaneously both to demystify the history of the West and to explore the possibilities of African-derived culture in post-modern society. In Reed's history, art plays a key role in the struggle between scientific and traditional systems of morality. Early in the history of the West scientific thinking shattered the unity of traditional society, represented for Reed by an idyllic vision of ancient Egypt.

> In Egypt at the time of Osiris every man was an artist and every artist a priest; it wasn't until later that art became attached to the state to do with it what it pleased.

What the state did with art was either to turn it into propaganda or to seal it off from political life through the ideology of High Art, both moves serving to bolster a social order that justifies state rule.

Far more interesting to Reed than an explicitly propagandistic use of art is the cultural imperialism involved in the attempt to generalize Western autonomous art as universal High Art. Since the Atonists define the dominant culture and control its dissemination through print and electronic media, it is the European classics that are held up as "the most notable achievements of mankind." Art museums—Centers of Art Detention—serve to enforce a useless kind of aesthetic autonomy, separating both the Western classics and "primitive" art from social praxis. The novel explores two contradictory methods of liberating art from detention, philosophies of avant-garde praxis that represent the two paths open to African-American literature, both in the twenties, the time of the Jes Grew story, and in the seventies at the time of Reed's own writing.

The first method of artistic liberation involves the physical removal of Third World artworks from Western museums by a multicultural gang of artnappers, who represent a strategy of using violence against the established order. They use people as tools in their projects, as when they kidnap Musclewhite, the director of the Center of Art Detention, in order to get a Toltec head for ransom, and by so doing they practice the instrumental and violent morality developed by Atonism itself. Thus discredited, violent separatist cultural activism takes a back seat to an explicitly non-instrumental practice whose spokesman within the novel is Papa LaBas, and whose model is the synchronic practice of Reed's own novelistic strategy in *Mumbo Jumbo*.

The novel's self-assertion as social praxis relies on the avant-garde negations of art that constitute Reed's text. Aside from deconstructing the conventions of literary realism, a move that postmodernism inherits from modernism, *Mumbo Jumbo* departs from even the modernist novel through its use of discursive forms from outside the genre. The addition of illustrations, footnotes, and a bibliography to its fictional text situates *Mumbo Jumbo* between novelistic, academic, and print media discourse. The "Partial Bibliography" at the end of the book stands out as a key avant-gardist device with several functions. Aside from challenging genre expectations and complicating the distinction between fiction and fact, the bibliography plays another, contradictory role. The placement of a bibliography at the end of a fictional text certainly parodies both scholarly claims to authority, as [critic Henry Louis] Gates [Jr.] notes and the literary use of cultural documentation by the white modernism of T.S. Eliot and Ezra Pound. But, at the same time, the bibliography attempts to do real historical and anthropological recovery work, harnessing the prestige of academic knowledge to support its critique of rationalism and its promotion of the African-American narrative tradition.

Reed insists on the need for African-American culture to maintain all its traditional sensuality and to resist the pressures of Western instrumental reason and pragmatism in general, but within the post-industrial West in which it has been placed, and not in a quixotic return to pre-modern idyllic unity. In the modified speech-act terminology of Jean-Francois Lyotard's theory of society in *The Postmodern Condition* (1979), black culture for Reed is a separate "language game" from white culture, a body of knowledge with different rules and different criteria for determining value. For Reed, black culture is what Lyotard defines as traditional or narrative culture, a fluid social arrangement that thrives on many kinds of knowledge, all of which seek an egalitarian encounter with nature and with people in society. In the industrial age narrative is opposed to science, the positivistic quest for mastery that characterizes dominant white culture for Reed.

The encounter of modern science with narrative is for Lyotard an unequal one, which explains the failure of Jes Grew to generalize itself at the end of Reed's tale. This inequality is due to the relative openness of narrative over science; while traditional narrative culture tolerates all sorts of knowledge, even science itself, scientific enlightenment on the other hand denounces narratives as archaic mystifications, "fables, myths [and] legends, fit only for women and children." Like Reed, Lyotard sees this "unequal relationship . . . [as] the entire history of cultural imperialism from the dawn of Western civilization." The history of cultural domination recounted in *Mumbo Jumbo* is the antagonism between positivism, geared toward efficiency, and narrative culture where people and things are not means but ends in themselves.

However, this antagonism obtains only for positivism, the scientific discourse of the industrial modern period whose goal is efficiency. In postmodernity, Lyotard claims the dominant mode of science is not logical but "paralogical," relying not on a universal system of rationality based on consistency and identity, but on local explanations that take account of paradoxes and indeterminacy. This postmodern thinking is realized today in disciplines like quantum physics and catastrophe theory and microphysics that undertake not only to question and revise previous scientific knowledge, but to challenge the very category of science itself and its separation from narrative.

This is a very avant-garde move, and it parallels the challenge to Western rationalistic culture made by Reed. Yet, here we see that what was in one sense an avant-garde revolt on Reed's part was also an assertion of a certain kind of aesthetic autonomy from social praxis. In the Atonist-dominated world of *Mumbo Jumbo* the whole spectrum of social praxis, from repatriating Third World art to invading Haiti, is governed by bourgeois rationalism and the modern drive toward efficiency. Thus, all pragmatic measures use people as instruments, making them into various means towards various ends. To resist dominant reason, Reed insists on the autonomy of his text from achievable political programs. Like Lyotard, Reed sees modern science and narrative as two separate language games, with different rules for validity. Only when society abandons the drive toward mastery and efficiency, and makes a space for paradox, can Reed envision the congruity of science and narrative, and consequently, of black and white. Until then, if "then" ever comes, art must stand in a critical relation to society, and African-American culture must lead the way to a democratic and pluralist postmodernism.

If on a winter's night a traveler and Metafiction

Salman Rushdie

Perhaps best known for the controversy surrounding his novel *The Satanic Verses,* Salman Rushdie is also the author of six other novels, a collection of short stories, and numerous essays on literature. This selection is taken from a 1981 review of one of the cornerstone novels of postmodernism, *If on a winter's night a traveler* by Italo Calvino. Rushdie has cited Calvino as an important influence on his own writing, as have Umberto Eco and John Barth. His discussion of Calvino's most famous novel centers on the playful ways in which Calvino manipulates his story (or stories). *If on a winter's night a traveler* is a prime example of metafiction—a sub-genre closely associated with postmodernism. Metafiction is fiction that is concerned primarily with the process of its own making. *If on a winter's night a traveler* intentionally confuses imagination and reality to such an extent as to call even its own existence into question, an ironic situation that is inherently postmodern.

At the beginning of Italo Calvino's first book for six years, an entirely fictional personage named You, the Reader, buys and settles down with a novel which he firmly believes to be the new Calvino. 'You prepare to recognize the unmistakable tone of the author. No. You don't recognize it at all. But now that you think about it, who ever said this author had an unmistakable tone? On the contrary, he is known as an author who changes greatly from one book to the next.' One of the difficulties with writing about Italo Calvino is that he has already said about himself just about everything there is to be said.

If on a winter's night a traveler distils into a single volume what is perhaps the dominant characteristic of Calvino's en-

tire output: his protean, metamorphic genius for never doing the same thing twice. In the space of 260 pages, we are
given the beginnings of no fewer than ten novels, each of
which is a transmogrified avatar of the previous one; we
also have a more or less fully developed love story between
the above-mentioned You and Ludmilla, the Other Reader;
plus, for good measure, a conspiracy-theory fiction about a
secret organization known as the Organization of Apoc-
ryphal Power, run by a fiendish translator named Ermes
Marana, whose purpose may or may not be the subversion
of fiction itself. The OAP is vaguely reminiscent of Thomas
Pynchon's underground postal service [from *The Crying of
Lot 49*], the Tristero System, and almost certainly has covert
links with [Luis] Buñuel's Revolutionary Army of the Infant
Jesus, the only comic terrorist organization in the history of
the cinema. (Buñuel's film *The Phantom of Liberty*, with its
almost infinite sequence of plots which take over the movie,
one after the other, with astonishing casualness, and are
then themselves supplanted with hilarious ease, is the work
of art which most closely resembles *If . . .*)

It is entirely possible that Calvino is not a human being at
all, but a planet, something like the planet Solaris of Stanis-
law Lem's great novel. Solaris, like Calvino, possesses the
power of seeing into the deepest recesses of human minds
and then bringing their dreams to life. Reading Calvino, you
are constantly assailed by the notion that he is writing down
what you have always known, except that you've never
thought of it before. . . .

CALVINO'S MASTERPIECE OF POSTMODERNISM

If on a winter's night a traveler, however, is a book to praise
without buts. This is Calvino rampant in the world of books,
Calvino joyously playing with the possibilities of fiction, of
story-telling, which is, after all, also a nursery euphemism
for lying; You, the Reader, is (or are) a sort of dogged Lemmy
Caution figure [the hero of Jean Luc Goddard's film *Alpha-
ville*] trying to find Your way through the literary labyrinths
of Calvino's city of words, his Alphabetaville.

You buy 'the new Calvino'. You begin reading a story
called 'If on a winter's night a traveler'. (I note that an 'I' has
fallen out of this last word in its journey from the dust-
jacket.) The story is a thriller set at a train station. But suddenly You have to stop reading: there is a binding error in

Your copy. You take it back to the bookshop and find that the story You began wasn't the new Calvino at all. The wrong pages, the bookseller tells You, were bound between the wrong covers. What You started (and now want to finish) was *Outside the town of Malbork* by one Tazio Bazakbal. You, and Your new friend Ludmilla, who has had the same problem with her copy of the Calvino, go off to read this second book. But it turns out to be an entirely different story, some kind of rural novel, and then another binding mistake is discovered just when You're getting interested: blank pages have been bound in by mistake. You ring Ludmilla, speak first to her sister Lotaria, eventually to this girl in whom You have become very interested indeed. You find that what you believed to be *Outside the town of Malbork* is in fact (another publisher's cock-up) a part of an old book written in Cimmerian, the language of an extinct East European culture. You go off to Professor Uzzi-Tuzii at the University and he tells You the original was called *Leaning from a steep slope*. Painfully, he begins to translate for you. Then he gets more and more fluent as the story weaves its spell. It is, of course, a completely different story, nothing to do with Malbork, about a young man of excessive soulfulness who gets caught up in a prison escape plot. Suddenly Uzzi-Tuzii stops reading. He tells You that the author, Ukko Ahti, committed suicide after reaching this point in the story. But now Lotaria appears with one Galligani, Professor of Erulo-Altaic languages. Galligani, an enemy of Uzzi-Tuzii's, claims that *Leaning from a steep slope* is in fact derived from a Cimbrian original, *Without fear of wind or vertigo,* by Vorts Viljandi.

Without fear, etc., turns out to be yet another, and completely unrelated work, about spies and counterspies in a city in the throes of a coup. But again, only a fragment remains, because Lotaria has given away most of the pages.

Two things need to be said right away: first, that all the fragments are wonderfully readable, and somehow don't seem fragmentary at all; second, that You, the Reader, have been getting less and less peripheral, and Your involvement with Ludmilla and Lotaria more and more important.

You now cease to be merely a passive reader. You act. You go to the publishers themselves, determined to find a copy of *Without fear of wind or vertigo,* which is what you now want to continue with. Here you meet Mr Cavedagna, who speaks, for the first time, the ominous name of Ermes Marana, translator, who has apparently been passing off as Polish, Cimmerian, Cimbrian what is actually a Belgian novel, *Looks down in the gathering shadow,* by Bertrand Vandervelde. You go off to read this new book, which inevitably bears no relationship to any of the other fragments you've seen, but is so exciting that it doesn't matter. *Looks down . . .* is a sort of film noir spoof, about a crook and his moll trying to get rid of a body in a plastic bag. You (the real you this time) will probably agree with You (not the real . . .) and Ludmilla that this is the most gripping thing you've read yet. But this, too, breaks off . . . Cavedagna hasn't lent You the whole typescript. You return to see him. 'Ah,' he tells You, 'Heaven knows where it's got to.'

Now, in despair, Cavedagna shows You the file on Ermes Marana, who has managed to throw the entire affairs of this publishing house into turmoil . . . and, because I don't want to give away the whole plot, I will content myself with telling you that there are five more extracts from stories, and that the story of You, Ludmilla and Lotaria now becomes deeply embroiled in the fictions You are trying to read.

Inventiveness That Is Never Tiresome

If on a winter's night a traveler is quite possibly the most complicated book you (and You, too) will ever read. But Calvino's conjuring trick works because he makes the complications so funny, and makes you (though not You) share the joke. The ten transformations of the eternally beginning story are carried off with an inventiveness that never becomes tiresome; the gradual inweaving of the texts and their readers is nothing less than—to use an appropriately archaic piece of slang—wizard. Calvino has left Stevenson far behind; he has avoided sounding like imitation Borges, which is what happens to him when he isn't on peak form; and his great gift, the ability to give credibility to the most extravagant of his inventions, has never been more in evidence. In *If . . .* , the most outrageous fiction about fiction ever conceived, we stumble in every paragraph over nuggets of hard, irreducible truth:

> 'Nobody these days holds the written word in such high esteem as police states do,' Arkadian Porphyrich says. 'What statistic allows one to identify the nations where literature enjoys true consideration better than the sums appropriated for controlling it and suppressing it?'

Why, finally, should we bother with a Calvino, a word-juggler, a fantasist? ... Not [for] escapism, because although the reader of Italo Calvino will be taken further out of himself than most readers, he will also discover that the experience is not a flight from, but an enrichment of himself. No, the reason why Calvino is such an indispensable writer is precisely that he tells us, joyfully, wickedly, that there are things in the world worth loving as well as hating; and that such things exist in people, too. I can think of no finer writer to have beside me while Italy explodes, while Britain burns, while the world ends.

Angela Carter: The Difficulty of Defining a Postmodernist

Aidan Day

Among the adjectives that have been used to describe Angela Carter's writing are "mythical", "magical", "Gothic", "fantastic", "feminist", "dreamlike", and "postmodern". Aidan Day, professor of English Literature at the University of Edinburgh in Scotland, claims that each of these is problematic in describing her work. Departing from the general critical opinion, Day sees her as a "fundamentally anti-postmodern" writer in spite of her extensive study of a number of the foremost French theoreticians of postmodernism. He defends his position by cataloging a number of views on Carter that he claims are more concerned with "claiming" her for a particular school of thought than with accurately representing her work. Day claims that Carter's gender politics and insistence on rationalism place her in opposition to the dominant postmodernist thought of her time. Since postmodernism has often been accused of being a male-dominated philosophy, inclusion of clearly feminist writers such as Carter or Kathy Acker within this category of framework is often problematic, since it often presents seeming conflicts of interest.

Carter's fiction is a bit extreme. She explores aspects of Western sexuality through a series of strange fables: about a doctor who invents reality-distorting machines, a man who is surgically transformed into a *Playboy* centrefold, a woman who grows wings, and so on. Her style is vivid, highly wrought. Some readers flinch from this manner, though I happen to find it thrilling. Thrilling and—very often—amusing. In a per-

ceptive review of *Shaking a Leg,* Carter's collected journalism, Blake Morrison noted that 'Her power as a feminist
writer is that she's funny and derisive'. Carter's mocking and
subversive humour can be felt throughout her fiction, where
she frequently uses it against the most unhumorous of objects. Humour directed towards sometimes deadly serious
ends is a Carter forte. It is an aspect of the zeal that drives her
style. In an interview published in 1985 John Haffenden said
to Carter: 'I think it's true that you do embrace opportunities
for overwriting'. To which Carter replied: 'Embrace them? I
would say that I half-suffocate them with the enthusiasm
with which I wrap my arms and legs around them'. . . . I must
say I sympathise with Carter's unashamed endorsement of
her own manner. Sympathetic readers have found many different ways of describing the special character of Carter's
work. 'Undecorous, overripe and mocking tales in which
nothing is sacred and nothing natural', says Nicci Gerrard.
Lorna Sage writes that Carter's fictions

> prowl around on the fringes of the proper English novel like
> dream-monsters—nasty, erotic, brilliant creations that feed off
> cultural crisis. She has taken over the sub-genres (romance,
> spies, porn, crime, gothic, science fiction) and turned their
> grubby stereotypes into sophisticated mythology . . . she writes
> aggressively against the grain of puritanism-cum-naturalism,
> producing adult fairy tales.

Marina Warner has observed that Carter's

> imagination was one of the most dazzling this century, and
> through her daring, vertiginous plots, her precise yet wild im-
> agery, her gallery of wonderful bad-good girls, beasts, rogues
> and other creatures, she causes readers to hold their breath
> as a mood of heroic optimism forms against the odds.

'Tales in which nothing is . . . natural', 'dream-monsters',
'daring, vertiginous plots': the anti-realism of Carter's dominant style has generated a rash of more technical labellings.
Carter is a 'magic realist' or she is a 'postmodernist'; she is a
writer of 'speculative fiction' or she is a writer of 'fantastic
fiction'. More on this kind of terminology later: for the moment I must note that Carter's antirealism has also provoked
a special form of mythologising, a mythologising that con-
founds author and work.

This mythologising is especially apparent in some of the
obituaries and other retrospective pieces written after
Carter's death on 16 February 1992. Many of Carter's obituaries were deeply felt and deeply moving. Margaret Atwood,

for example, in a piece that acutely registers her sense of loss, observed that the 'imagination at work' in Carter's writing 'was mercurial, multi-sided, and more than faintly Gothic'. But she also spoke of Carter's appearance and personality, if not in terms of the Gothic, then at least in those of the fairy tale:

> The amazing thing about her, for me, was that someone who looked so much like the Fairy Godmother . . . should actually *be* so much like the Fairy Godmother. She seemed always on the verge of bestowing something—some talisman, some magic token. . . . There was something of *Alice*'s White Queen about her, too.

In a comparable vein, the presenter of a BBC2 television memorial to Carter (*The Late Show*, 18 February 1992), spoke of her as the 'white witch of English Literature'. Some three years after Carter's death Nicci Gerrard was to observe, in an appreciation in *The Observer*, that Carter

> has achieved a cult status: the good witch, the fairy godmother, the Gothic fabulist of English fiction. And she looked a bit like a fairy godmother, with her large-boned height, prematurely white mane of hair, pink skin and far-seeing, blinky, ever-so-knowing eyes.

RESISTING THE MYTHMAKER LABEL

The problems with this cult were highlighted, not long after Carter's obituaries appeared, by Merja Makinen: 'this concurrence of white witch/fairy godmother mythologising needs watching; it is always the dangerously problematic that are mythologised in order to make them less dangerous'. There is a particular irony about Carter and her work being mythologised. She was herself so anti-mythic. 'A lot of my conscious energy', she observed in 1984, 'is devoted to demythologising things'. A year earlier, in an essay entitled 'Notes from the Front Line', she had written:

> I become mildly irritated (I'm sorry!) when people, as they sometimes do, ask me about the 'mythic quality' of work I've written lately. Because I believe that all myths are products of the human mind and reflect only aspects of material human practice. I'm in the demythologising business.

Carter expanded a little on this in a 1988 interview with Anna Katsavos:

> AK: In 'Notes From the Front Line' you say that you are not in the remythologising business but in the 'demythologising business'. What exactly do you mean?

AC: Well, I'm basically trying to find out what certain configurations of imagery in our society, in our culture, really stand for, what they mean, underneath the kind of semireligious coating that makes people not particularly want to interfere with them.

AK: In what sense are you defining myth?

AC: In a sort of conventional sense; also in the sense that Roland Barthes uses it in *Mythologies*—ideas, images, stories that we tend to take on trust without thinking what they really mean.

Not thinking what Carter's own stories really mean, not thinking about their demythologising energy, may apply also to some of the readers of those stories. Nicci Gerrard writes: 'I remember a colleague of mine'—who was idealis-

POSTMODERNISM AS SOCIAL PROTEST

Until her death in 1997 at the age of forty-nine, Kathy Acker consistently injected an uncompromisingly radical viewpoint into postmodernism. Her work, both as a critic and an author of fiction, is controversial for its unusual style and confrontational politics. This brief excerpt demonstrates Acker's belief that postmodernism is not just an inventive aesthetic movement but also a countercultural social philosophy.

I write with words which are given me. If it wasn't for certain community consensus as to the meanings and usages of words, words would be nonsense. Language, then, deeply is discourse: when I use language, I am given meaning and I give meaning back to the community. "Culture" is one way by which a community attempts to bring its past up out of senselessness and to find in dream and imagination possibilities for action. When culture isn't this, there's something wrong in the community, the society.

Political, economic and moral forces are major determiners of meanings and values in a society. Thus, when I use words, any words, I am always taking part in the constructing of the political, economic, and moral community in which my discourse is taking place. All aspects of language—denotation, sound, style, syntax, grammar, etc.—are politically, economically and morally coded. In this sense, there's no escaping content. Whenever someone, the literati, the professors, declares that there is such a thing as "total ornament," that "art is pure," what they are saying is that the rich own culture, discourse, and probably the world. If this seems like a non

ing or mythologising Carter 'as a New Age role model, an earth mother'—'once asking Carter to write something on the summer solstice and Stonehenge; Carter looked at her pityingly and said in her soft, reedy voice: "You just haven't got me, have you dear?"' Carter's view was that myth functions to console people—not least, women—for deprivation and dissatisfaction in the actual world:

> All the mythic versions of women, from the myth of the redeeming purity of the virgin to that of the healing, reconciling mother, are consolatory nonsenses; and consolatory nonsense seems to me a fair definition of myth, anyway . . .
>
> Myth deals in false universals, to dull the pain of particular circumstances.

To mythologise Carter and her writing is indeed to neu-

---

sequitur, you figure it out.

Whenever I engage in discourse, I am using given meanings and values, changing them and giving them back. A community, a society is always being constructed in discourse if and when discourse—including art—is allowed. Societies whose economies are set, fascist ones for instance, place little or no emphasis on free discourse, on art. Of course art, then, is trivial. The rich want to stay rich.

Language always occurs in the present because it makes the present, because it's active.

We are now, in the United States and in England, living in a world in which ownership is becoming more and more set: The rich stay rich; the poor stay dead. Death-in-life. The only social mobility left occurs in terms of appearance: things no longer change hands. But fashion is not purely ornamental: it is political. All signs nowadays point either to the world of the "haves" or to the homeless Chicanos on the L.A. downtown streets. There is no more right-wing versus working class: there is only appearance and disappearance, those people who appear in the media and those people who have disappeared from the possibility of any sort of home. In such a society as ours the only possible chance for change, for mobility, for political, economic, and moral flow lies in the tactics of guerrilla warfare, in the use of fictions, of language.

Postmodernism, then, for the moment, is a useful perspective and tactic. If we don't live for and in the, this, moment, we do not live.

Kathy Acker, "Postmodernism" in *Bodies of Work: Essays*. New York: Serpent's Tail, 1997, pp. 4–5.

tralise the dangerous relevance to life of her life's work. Given the flamboyance and sheer outrageousness of much of her writing, it is perhaps not surprising that Carter and her work have been mythologised. Even so, Marina Warner's obituary *was* able to keep a steady eye on the referents of Carter's fantasies. Warner's obituary makes the one move that the mythologisers do not when she points out that 'For a fantasist, Carter kept her feet on the ground. . . . For her fantasy always turns back its eyes to stare hard at reality, never losing sight of material conditions'. . . .

CARTER AND THE EARLY POSTMODERNIST CRITICS

Carter's materialist metaphysic . . . conditioned her attitude to the philosophical and theoretical issues of her times. She was well read in the cultural, political and literary theories of writers like Barthes, Theodor Adorno and Michel Foucault. Lorna Sage has noted that:

> Her closest affinities earlier on had probably been with Roland Barthes, but in the 1970s it was, I suspect, Michel Foucault who counted most. She lists his early book *Madness and Civilization* (1961) in [*The Sadeian Woman's*] bibliography, but she was also thinking very much along the same lines as he had in *La Volonté de savoir* (1976), translated as Volume I of *The History of Sexuality* in 1978 . . . like her, he's concerned to question the notion that sex is outside history: 'what was involved . . . was the very production of sexuality. Sexuality must not be thought of as a kind of natural given which power tries to hold in check, or as an obscure domain which knowledge tries gradually to uncover. It is the name that can be given to an historical construct: not a furtive reality that is difficult to grasp, but a great surface network in which the stimulation of bodies, the intensification of pleasures, the incitement to discourse . . . are linked to one another, in accordance with a few major strategies of knowledge and power.' Carter's 'Flesh comes to us out of history' *(The Sadeian Woman)* makes the same move.

Carter's reading of people like Barthes and Foucault can be felt throughout her stories ('my fiction is very often a kind of literary criticism', she observed to John Haffenden). But her materialism and her political engagement led her to be suspicious of some of the avant-garde tendencies of thought which came to the fore in the 1960s and after. She came to be uneasy with the postmodern idea that authors have no unmediated access to a reality outside of language and texts. At the heart of that unease lay the vexed question of the relations between postmodern thought and political engagement. For several years, Carter told Kerryn Goldsworthy in 1985:

> I thought that writing, all fiction, really, was about other fiction. That there was no way out, really, of this solipsism; that books were about other books . . .
>
> But then I began to ask myself, if all books are about other books, what are the other books about? . . . What's the Ur-book, then? And one is forced to answer, after a while, of course the Ur-book is really Life, or The Real World . . .
>
> One of the things that really made me feel that a whole lot of the post-modernists were sort of tap-dancing on the edge of the abyss was reading Christina Stead, which I did very recently, three or four years ago. I read almost all her novels at a gulp. And I thought—my goodness me, there's an awful lot of life left in the old horse yet . . .
>
> All the interviews I've read with her in her old age are so equivocal. I mean she really isn't interested in telling everybody—she's lying all the time. She seems to have acute paranoia about most of her past. . . . She was blacklisted in Hollywood. . . . And you get absolute idiots asking her things like, 'Were you interested in politics?'

There are many ways of reading Carter. . . . Major aspects of Carter's metaphysical materialism are her empiricism and her passion for reason. Carter's exploration, throughout her fantastic allegories, of 'Life, or The Real World' is primarily an exploration of the politics of Western heterosexual identity. But . . . this exploration is conducted through an engagement with the discourses of reason. Carter's wild fables and the pungency of her style may disguise the extent to which her feminism is grounded in the values of reason. 'Reason' is not, of course, a neutral term and . . . her vision significantly modifies the Enlightenment structuring of rationality. As Elaine Jordan has acutely observed, Carter 'is . . . great in rethinking the fables of Enlightened modernity'. . . . In her rationality, Carter stands at odds with an extreme postmodernism: not postmodernism as defined simply by formal textual features such as pastiche, intertextuality or reflexiveness (some, at least, of such features arguably appear in modernist and earlier texts as well as in Carter); but postmodernism as defined also in a more philosophical sense. . . . Carter stands at odds with this latter sense of postmodernism because the relativising impulse of such postmodernism threatens to undermine the grounds of a liberal-rationalist, specifically feminist politics. Susan Rubin Suleiman has described Carter as a 'feminist postmodernist'. . . . Carter's fiction, principally because of its rationalist feminism, as fundamentally anti-postmodern.

Dictionary of the Khazars: Hypertextual Folklore

Angela Carter

Angela Carter was the author of nine novels and several collections of short stories that have been described as postmodern by a number of critics. In this selection, she discusses the Yugoslavian writer Milorad Pavic, whose 1988 novel *Dictionary of the Khazars* has become a classic of postmodernism. Carter describes this novel as both similar to traditional folklore and as a prototype of the free-flowing hypertext fiction that has sprung up with the popularization of the Internet. Although she never identifies the book specifically as postmodern herself, she lists a number of attributes of *Dictionary of the Khazars* that are central to postmodernism, including surrealism, playfulness, and self-referentiality.

The Yugoslav writer Milorad Pavic's *Dictionary of the Khazars* is an exercise in a certain kind of erudite frivolity that does not do you good *as such,* but offers the cerebral pleasure of the recognition of patterning afforded by formalism, a profusion of language games, some rude mirth. In culinary terms, the book is neither tofuburger nor Big Mac, but a Chinese banquet, a multiplicity of short narratives and prose fragments at which we are invited, not to take our fill, but to snack as freely or as meagrely as we please on a wide variety of small portions of sharply flavoured delicacies, mixing and matching many different taste sensations. . . . It will not set you up; nor will it tell you how to live. That is not what it is for.

The mother-type of these feast-like compilations is *The Arabian Nights Entertainment*—note the word 'entertainment'. That shambolic anthology of literary fairytales linked by an exiguous narrative was originally, and still is, related to the folktale of peasant communities and its particular improvisatory yet regulated systems of narrative. The whole of *Dictionary of the Khazars* is a kind of legendary history, and some of the individual entries have considerable affinities to the folktale ('The Tale of Petkutin and Kalina' in the section called 'The Red Book', for example): but, I suspect, not so much the influence of an oral tradition—though that's still possible in Yugoslavia—as the influence of an aesthetic owing a good deal to Vladimir Propp's *Morphology of the Folk-Tale,* first published in Russia in 1928.

SUPERFICIAL BUILDING BLOCKS OF FAIRYTALE NARRATIVE

Propp's thesis is that the traditional fairytale is not composed, but built up out of discrete narrative blocks that can be pulled down again and reassembled in different ways to make any number of other stories, or can be used for any number of other stories in combination with other narrative blocks. That is partly why there is no place for, nor possibility of, inwardness in the traditional tale, nor of characterisation in any three-dimensional way. If the European novel of the nineteenth and twentieth centuries is closely related to gossip, to narrative arising out of conflicted character, then the folktale survives, in our advanced, industrialised, society, in the anecdote. Gossip would say: 'You know the daughter of that bloke at the "Dog and Duck"? Well . . .' An anecdote might begin: 'There was this publican's daughter, see . . .' In our culture, the folktale survives in the saloon bar.

A traditional storyteller does not make things up afresh, except now and then, if the need arises. Instead, he or she selects, according to mood, whim and cultural background, the narrative segments that feel right at the time from a store acquired from a career of listening, and reassembles them in attractive, and sometimes new, ways. And that's how formalism was born. (Italo Calvino, the most exquisite of contemporary formalists, is also, it should be remembered, editor of the classic collection of Italian fairytales.)

Pavic advises the reader to behave exactly like a traditional storyteller and construct his or her own story out of the ample material he has made available. The main difference is, Pavic has made all this material up by himself. 'No chronology is observed here, nor is one necessary. Hence, each reader will put together the book for himself, as in a game of dominoes or cards.' The book is an exercise, not in creative writing, but in creative reading. The reader can, says Pavic, rearrange the book 'in an infinite number of ways, like a Rubic cube'.

Pavic positively invites you to join in, as if opening his imagination to the public. 'It is an open book,' he says in the preliminary notes, 'and when it is shut it can be added to: just as it has its own former and present lexicographer, so it can acquire new writers, compilers, continuers.'

In a US review, Robert Coover suggested that computer hackers might make *Dictionary of the Khazars* their own as a prototype hypertext, unpaginated, non-sequential, that can be entered anywhere by anybody. This looks forward to a Utopian, high-tech version of the oral tradition where machines do all the work whilst men and women unite in joyous and creative human pastimes. It is a prospect to make William Morris's mind reel, publishers quail.

But who are, or were, the Khazars? 'An autonomous and powerful tribe, a warlike and nomadic people who appeared from the East at an unknown date, driven by a scorching silence, and who, from the seventh to the tenth century, settled in the land between two seas, the Caspian and the Black.' As a nation, the Khazars no longer exist, and ceased to do so during the tenth century after 'their conversion from their original faith, unknown to us today, to one (again, it is not known which) of three known religions of the past and present—Judaism, Islam or Christianity.'

WHAT *DICTIONARY OF THE KHAZARS* CLAIMS TO BE

The *Dictionary* purports to be, with some additions, the reprint of an edition of a book published by the Pole, Joannes Daubmannus, in 1691, which was 'divided into three dictionaries: a separate glossary of Moslem sources on the Khazar question, an alphabetised list of materials drawn from Hebrew writings and tales, and a third dictionary compiled on the basis of Christian accounts of the Khazar question'. So the same characters and events are usually seen three times, each from the perspective of a different history and set of cultural traditions, and may be followed through the three books *cross-wise,* if you wish. The 'ancient' texts are organised according to the antiquarian interests of the seventeenth century. As in *The Arabian Nights,* an exiguous narrative set in the present day is interwoven throughout the three volumes of the dictionary and provides some sort of climax.

The most obvious immediate inspiration for this 'plot' is

surely a certain Volume XLVI of the *Anglo-American Cyclopaedia* (New York, 1917), itself a 'literal but delinquent reprint of the *Encyclopaedia Britannica* of 1902', in which Bioy Cesares and Jorge Luis Borges discovered the first recorded reference to the land of Uqbar. But instead of, like Borges, writing a story about a fake reference book that invades the real world, Pavic has set to and compiled the book itself, a book that contains a whole lost world, with its heroes, its rituals, its deaths, its mysteries, and especially its theological disputations, providing a plausible-enough-sounding apparatus of scholarly references that involve a series of implicit jokes about theories of authenticity just as the skewed versions of characters such as Princess Ateh, recurring three times, involve implicit jokes about cultural relativity.

Unless, of course, these aren't jokes at all. Yugoslavia is a federation of states with extraordinarily diverse cultural histories that came together as a nation almost by accident in 1918, with a sizeable Moslem population, to boot. This idea of a tripartite version of an imaginary history ought to appeal to the British, since the United Kingdom is also a union of principalities with extraordinarily diverse cultural histories, and a significant Moslem minority, too.

There is a blatant quality of fakery about the *Dictionary*. One imagines Pavic gleefully setting to with a Black and Decker drill, inserting artificial worm-holes into his synthetic oak beams. This fakery, this purposely antiqued and distressed surface, is what makes Pavic's book look so post-modern as to be almost parodically fashionable, the perfect type of those Euro-bestsellers such as Patrick Suskind's *Perfume* and Umberto Eco's *Name of the Rose* that seem, to some British critics, to spring from an EEC conspiracy to thwart exports of genuine, wholesome, straightforward British fiction the same way French farmers block the entry of English lamb. However, Yugoslavia is not a member of the Common Market and the British have developed a nervous tendency to label anything 'post-modern' that doesn't have a beginning, a middle, and an end in that order.

A SURREAL EXPERIENCE

In Yugoslavia, according to Martin Seymour-Smith, 'except for a few years after Tito came to power in 1945, Modernism has flourished almost, if not quite, as it wished' *(Guide to World Literature,* edition of 1985). *Dictionary of the Khazars* fulfils, almost too richly, all Wallace Stevens's prescriptions in 'Notes towards a Supreme Fiction':

    it must be abstract
    it must change
    it must give pleasure

Most of the time, Pavic speaks in the language of romantic modernism—that is, surrealism. Al Bakri, the Spaniard, dies 'dreaming of salty female breasts in a gravy of saliva and toothache'. The Princess Ateh composes a prayer: 'On our ship, my father, the crew swarms like ants: I cleaned it this morning with my hair and they crawl up the clean mast and strip the green sails like sweet vine leaves into their anthills.' A man, a certain Dr Ismail Suk, waking, blinks, 'with eyes hairy as testicles'.

Dr Suk is the hero of a section called 'The Story of the Egg and the Violin Bow' that boasts all the inscrutability of surrealist narrative plus a quality of what one can only call the 'mercantile fantastic' reminiscent of the short stories of Bruno Schulz, with their bizarre and ominous shops and shopkeepers. 'The shop was empty except for a hen nestled in a cap in the corner. She cocked one eye at Dr Suk and saw everything edible in him.' The Polish woman who will murder Dr Suk is called Dr Dorothea Schulz.

In fact, there is a strong sense of pastiche everywhere, most engagingly in the collection of Islamic sources on the Khazar question, although the poem in question purports to have been written by the Khazar princess Ateh. It is a piece of spoof Kafka. A woman travelling to a distant school to take a test is subjected to bureaucratic misinformation and then told: 'you can't reach the school today. And that means not ever. Because the school will no longer exist as of tomorrow. You have missed your life's destination . . .'

But this is a revisionist version of Kafka. Once her destination is withheld from her, the traveller searches for the significance of her journey in the journey itself—and finds it in one luminous memory, of a table with food and wine. 'On the table by the food a candle with a drop of flame on the top; next to it the Holy Book and the month of Jemaz-ul-Aker flowing through it.' A happy ending!

There is the casual acceptance of the marvellous common to both surrealism and the folktale: 'Ibn Ashkany was himself a very deft player. There exists a written record of his fingering for a song, so we know that he used more than ten fingers to play his instruments.' (In fact, Satan used this name for a time, and we learn how he played the lute with both his fingers and the tip of his tail.) A band of Greek merchants are 'so hirsute that the hair on their chests had a part like the hair on their heads'.

But the sense of the marvellous is most often created simply by the manipulation of language: 'Avram Brankovich cuts a striking figure. He has a broad chest the size of a cage for large birds or a small beast.' One way and another, the task of Pavic's translator, Christina Privicevic-Zoric, must have been awesome, for among the Khazars we are living in a world of words *as such*. The vanished world of the Khazars is constructed solely out of words. A dictionary itself is a book in which words provide the plot. The Khazars are nothing if not people of the Book, dithering as they did between the three great faiths, the sacred texts of Christianity, Islam, and Judaism. One of the copies of the 1691 edition of the *Dictionary*, we are told, was printed with a poisoned ink: 'The reader would die on the ninth page at the words *Verbum caro factum est.* ("The Word became Flesh.")' Almost certainly, something metaphysical is going on.

PLUNDERING THE DREAM STATE

The Khazars indefatigably enter that most metaphysical of states, dreaming. 'A woman was sitting by her fire, her kettle of broth babbling like bursting boils. Children were standing in line with their plates and dogs, waiting. She ladled out the broth to the children and animals and immediately Masudi knew that she was portioning out dreams from the kettle.'

The Dream Hunters are a set of Khazar priests. 'They could read other people's dreams, live and make themselves at home in them . . .' That is the Christian version. The Moslem Dictionary is more forthcoming: 'If all human dreams could be assembled together, they would form a huge man, a human being the size of a continent. This would not be just any man, it would be Adam Ruhani, the heavenly Adam, man's angel ancestor, of whom the imams speak.'

The book of Hebrew sources is most explicit:

> The Khazars saw letters in people's dreams, and in them they looked for primordial man, for Adam Cadmon, who was both man and woman and born before eternity. They believed that to every person belongs one letter of the alphabet, that each

of these letters constitutes part of Adam Cadmon's body on earth, and that these letters converge in people's dreams and come to life in Adam's body.

(I am not sure that Pavic thinks of Freud when he thinks of dreams.)

So we can construct our primal ancestor out of the elements of our dreams, out of the elements of the *Dictionary*, just as Propp thought that if one found sufficient narrative elements and combined them in the right order, one would be able to retell the very first story of all—'it would be possible to construct the archetype of the fairy tale not only schematically . . . but concretely as well.'

The Emotionless Postmodern World of *Fargo*

Steven Carter

The 1996 film *Fargo* was both a critical and commercial success for its makers, Joel and Ethan Coen. More than just a diverting comedy, though, *Fargo* is a statement about the time in which it was made, claims Steven Carter, professor of English at California State University at Bakersfield. The film's lackadaisical depiction of a number of violent crimes and the general lack of emotion on the part of its characters makes it an indictment of the "postmodern condition." The characters in *Fargo* are numbed to life by television and participate passively in their own dehumanization, themes that noted postmodernist critics like Jean Baudrillard have accentuated in their writings.

Fargo was filmed in color, and yet it's the absence of color—the bone-chilling whiteness of a Minnesota winter—that sets the movie's quirky tone from beginning to end. *Fargo*'s central subject is disparity:

Jean Lundegaard: Do you know what a disparity is?

Scotty Lundegaard (testily): Yeah!

So should *Fargo's* audience, by film's end. For everything in *Fargo* is out of sync: its title (all but the brief opening sequence takes place in Minnesota, not North Dakota); its off-beat names (Mike Yanagita, Reilly Diefenbach, Gaear Grimsrud, Shep Proudfoot); its weather ("It's a beautiful day," Police Chief Marge Gunderson declares, as "[outside it is snowing. The sky, the earth, the road—all white.]"); its appointments ("Shep said you'd be here at 7:30"; "Shep said 8:30"); its musical score (strains of a traditional Norwegian

Excerpted from "'Flare to White': *Fargo* and the Postmodern Turn," by Steven Carter, *Literature/Film Quarterly*, vol. 27, no. 4, October 1999. Copyright © 1999 Salisbury State University. Reprinted with permission from *Literature/Film Quarterly*.

folk tune interspersed with automobile door chimes and white noise from television sets); its opening text:

> This is a true story. The events depicted in this film took place in Minnesota in 1987. At the request of the survivors, the names have been changed. Out of respect for the dead, the rest has been told exactly as it occurred.

> Flare to white . . .

In his introduction to the filmscript of *Fargo*, Ethan Coen declares, "[*Fargo*] aims to be both homey and exotic, and pretends to be true." In fact the killings in *Fargo* didn't take place in Minnesota in 1987 or at any other time (wouldn't Minnesotans remember hearing about a notorious murderer putting his partner, an equally notorious murderer, into a wood chipper?). More to the point, no one in the film has an iota of respect for the dead. To be sure, the psychopath Gaear Grimsrud is indifferent to the plight of his victims, but so is Chief Marge Gunderson—Gunderson, who was described by one naive early reviewer as "the film's moral center." With the dead body of an unlucky eyewitness to one of Grimsrud's crimes in the background, the very pregnant Marge feels the need to puke, not from moral or physical revulsion but from morning sickness. "Well, that passed," she says cheerfully, rising. "Now I'm hungry again."

FARGO AND THE POSTMODERN REACTION TO MURDER

Fargo isn't a crime film, nor, strictly speaking, is it about crime. The brilliance of the film, rather, lies in its ability to critique a certain contemporary, or postmodern, response to the crime of murder. Consider the following parallel between the reactions of both good guys and bad guys to the freezing cold of a Minnesota February. When she arrives on the scene of the triple homicide, Chief Marge asks her deputy, "Where is everybody?", meaning the other deputies. The redoubtable Lou replies, "Well—it's cold, Margie." A few moments later, Marge concludes: "I guess the little guy sat in there [the highway patrolman's prowler] waitin' for his buddy t' come back." Lou replies, "Yah, would a been cold out here." In *Fargo*, both heroes and villains are willing to sacrifice the better angels of their nature in order to seek out a bit of warmth.

As for the highway patrolman shot in the head by Grimsrud, all Marge Gunderson can manage is, "Well, he's got his gun on his hip there, and he looked like a nice enough fella."

Ethan Coen's skillful use of grammatical parataxis in this line recalls Ernest Hemingway's short story "After the Storm":

> I said "Who killed him?" and he said "I don't know who killed him but he's dead all right," and it was dark and there was water standing in the street and no lights and windows broke and boats all up in the town and trees blown down. . . .

The effect of the coordinate *and*'s in both instances is to dramatize the uncaringness that dwells beneath the lexical surface of each character's speech. Like Hemingway's narrator who sees a dead person and a fallen tree as being essentially one and the same—e.g., as mere visual objects—so Marge Gunderson mentions the fallen patrolman's holstered gun and his nice looks in the same breath. Like the narrator of "After the Storm," in other words, she can only respond esthetically, not emotionally, to suffering and death. Ultimately, Marge is as uncomprehending and unfeeling as one of her husband Norm's wooden duck decoys. When she gets to her feet after examining the dead trooper's body, she asks her deputy,

> Marge: Lou: Ya think, is Dave open yet?
> Lou: You don't think he's mixed up in—.
> Marge: No, no. I just wanna get Norm some night crawlers.

Marge's lack of comprehension reemerges near the very end of the film as she lectures the captured Grimsrud:

> And for what? . . . For a little bit of money. . . .
> There's more to life than a little bit of money,
> you know. . . . I just don't understand it.

Two jump cuts later, we are with Marge and Norm in bed:

> Marge: They announced it?
> Norm: Yah . . . Three cent stamp.
> Marge: Your mallard?
> Norm: Yah.
> Marge: Norm, that's terrific!
> Norm: It's just the three cent. . . . Hautman's blue-winged teal got the twenty-nine cent. People don't much use the three cent.
> Marge: Oh, for Pete's—a course they do! Every time they raise the darned postage, people need the little stamps!

This from the same woman who told Grimsrud a few screen seconds before, "There's more to life than a little bit of money."

Note too the callous Wade Gustafson wincing sharply as he watches Minnesota give up a goal during a televised hockey game with the University of Wisconsin. Later in the film, when Wade is mortally shot by Carl Showalter, he hardly winces at all, looking merely puzzled and emitting the mildest of "Ooooohs" as he falls to the ground. The emotion he displays while watching his favorite team lose a hockey game on TV is more deeply felt, more authentic, than the emotion he feels upon losing his life. (Showalter, on the other hand, reacts to being shot in a much more normal manner than does Wade; Showalter screams, flies into a rage, shoots Wade several more times, then kicks the lifeless body.)

In fact, only the abnormal characters—i.e., the bad guys—appear capable of expressing genuine human feeling in *Fargo*'s topsy-turvy world. The horny Carl Showalter is also lonely and continually berates his associate Grimsrud for not talking to him ("Would it kill you to say something?"); Shep Proudfoot, enraged because Showalter has jeopardized his parole from prison, gives him a vicious beating; Jerry Lundegaard screams hysterically upon being captured by the police. Even Grimsrud shows anger on occasion, as when he shouts "Shut the fuck up!" at Jean Lundegaard. Contrast these expressions of feeling with the barely audible whimpers emitted by the kidnapped Jean and the flat affect of Norm, Marge Gunderson's zombie-like husband.

LACK OF EMOTION AS PART OF "THE POSTMODERN CONDITION"

The Coen brothers are the latest in a long line of artists in fiction and film—the novelist Don DeLillo and the film-maker Quentin Tarantino come immediately to mind—to document the common inability of ordinary people of our era to feel passionately about anything. Fredric Jameson diagnoses this fashionable form of postmodern anomie as waning of affect:

> As for expression and feelings or emotions, the liberation, in contemporary society, from the older anomie of the centered subject may also mean not merely a liberation from anxiety but a liberation from every other kind of feeling as well, since there is no longer a self present to do the feeling. . . .

Another theorist, communications scholar Joshua Meyrowitz, links waning of affect directly to media overexposure:

> If we celebrate our child's wedding in an isolated [e.g., media-less] situation where it is the sole "experience" of the day, then our joy may be unbounded. But when, on our way to the wedding, we hear over the car radio of a devastating earthquake, or the death of a popular entertainer, or the as-

sassination of a political figure, we not only lose our ability to rejoice fully, but also our ability to mourn deeply. . . . As situations merge, the hot flush and the icy stare blend into a middle region 'cool.'

The merging of human situations into a middle region cool takes a number of forms in *Fargo*. Central to the film, for example, is the role of television. . . . Snow comes in two forms in *Fargo:* as natural and as televisual. One dominates the film's outdoor settings, the other its indoor settings. As Showalter cajoles and threatens the recalcitrant TV as if it were a person, the camera switches to the frozen stare of Grimsrud across the room. Like the television, the sullen, inhuman Grimsrud is quite incapable of responding to Showalter.

In another scene, Showalter and Grimsrud and their nightly pickups occupy adjoining beds as they watch *The Tonight Show;* later in the film we see Marge and Norm Gunderson in identical postures, lying next to each other in bed watching a nature program. All six characters appear to be rendered equally insensate by the ghostly, flickering images on the screen. I'll return to the Gundersons' nature program, an episode from the PBS series *Nova*, later on.

Television also helps to blur the moral distinctions between reality and simulacra in *Fargo*. In the film's least understood scene, Mike Yanagita, a high school chum of Marge Gunderson, meets her for a drink in the Twin Cities. (Some reviewers felt that the Coens should have left this bizarre *interregnum* on the cutting room floor. In fact, the appearance of Yanagita is a brilliant stroke: as a mentally disturbed Japanese-American who speaks with a Minnesota accent, he's the quintessence of disparity in *Fargo's* quirky universe: a walking, talking *mise en scene*.) When Yanagita tells Marge, "I saw you on the TV," we're being set up for a parallel moment that comes late in the film as Grimsrud, watching a barely discernible ("*suffused by snow*") soap opera on TV, hears a female character announce to her lover, "I'm pregnant." As two-dimensional simulacra—as humans who simply go through the motions of feeling and acting—the pregnant Marge and the TV actress are clear counterparts.

Fargo's most carefully crafted scene occurs when Showalter and Grimsrud kidnap Jean Lundegaard. As Jean watches an insipid morning show featuring a simulacrum-sun flaming in the background (see below), a stranger suddenly appears on the deck outside the full-length window. Jean turns her gaze from the TV screen to the other screen of glass as Showalter, wearing a ski mask and carrying a crowbar, peers inside. Watching this real intruder with the same blank stare that she gave the images on television a moment before, she is transfixed, registering absolutely no emotion. This frozen moment lasts a full five seconds—a cinemagraphic eternity. Only when Showalter shatters the glass and breaks through the screen—i.e., *becomes real*—does she react, and by then it's too late. Like her callous father, she's too desensitized by television to react appropriately, in normal human fashion, to a life-threatening situation.

Even as Showalter shatters and steps through the glass, so do other simulacra in *Fargo* unsettlingly come to life. One of the film's most arresting images is the huge wooden statue, located on the outskirts of Brainerd, Minnesota, of Paul Bunyan wielding an ax. This simulacrum is replicated in the person of the very tall Grimsrud, who buries an ax in Showalter's neck at the end of the film. In like manner, pint-sized golf enthusiast Jerry Lundegaard is replicated by the miniature wooden statue of a golfer on his desk at the car dealership (Lundegaard also wears an Elmer Fudd hat in one scene). And when the young hooker from White Bear Lake is asked to describe Grimsrud, she compares him to the Marlboro Man, an American simulacrum almost as mythopoetic as Paul Bunyan. Even the accordion-playing Scotty Lundegaard is identified with a two-dimensional simulacrum. In the one brief scene devoted to Scotty's bedroom, the camera lingers for a moment on the photograph of an adult "Accordion King" on the door, suggesting that Scotty will grow up to be like his parents: a pastiche of a person. In these and in other ways, then, *Fargo* deliberately erases the moral boundaries between humans and objects. These erasures project in visual terms the waning of affect that characterizes the empty inner lives of many of the film's characters.

ANIMAL METAPHORS IN *FARGO*

When writers of poetry, drama, and fiction wish to make a statement about inhumanity, they rarely do so directly; instead, they often encode their texts with symbolic animal imagery and/or motifs. When, for instance, Homer's Circe turns Odysseus' men into swine, the poet is "telling us" that they already *are* swine for having gorged themselves on the forbidden cattle of the sun. The purpose of the well-documented beast imagery in Shakespeare's *King Lear* is to raise the play's central question: is there, *au fond,* any difference between man and beast? Thus, Lear's anguished line spoken to Edgar, "Thou art the thing itself; unaccommodated man is no more but such a poor, bare, forked animal as thou art," is balanced by, "Why should a dog, a horse, a rat, have life,/And thou no breath at all?" spoken to the dead Cordelia.

In *The Great Gatsby,* F. Scott Fitzgerald introduces us to the guests who came to Gatsby's parties:

> . . . the Leeches . . . Doctor Webster Civet . . . Edgar Beaver . . . the Hammerheads . . . Cecil Roebuck . . . James B. ("Rot-Gut") Ferret . . . a man named Klipspringer [a small African antelope] . . . George Duckweed . . . Francis Bull . . .

These are the shameless people who get drunk on Gatsby's liquor and then fail to show up at his funeral. To indicate that love of money, power and fame has stripped them of their humanity, Fitzgerald appropriately assigns them animal names. Gatsby's parties are, in other words, so many moral menageries.

So far as I know, Joel and Ethan Coen are the first to adapt this fundamental literary method to an American film. And they do so in a literary way, embedding references to animals throughout the film's dialogue. On two occasions, however, we actually see lower forms of life. Both are disgusting:

Marge: Hiya, Hon.

She slides [a] paper sack toward [Norm].

Norm: Brought ya some lunch, Margie. What're those, night crawlers?

He looks inside. The bottom of the sack is full of fat, crawling earthworms.

A few screen minutes later, we are in the Gundersons' bedroom, watching them watch TV:

TV Voice-Over: The bark beetle carries the worm to the nest . . . where it will feed its young for up to six weeks . . .

From the TV set we hear insects chirring.

Like that of television, the function of the film's animal motif is to erase conventional moral boundaries between normal and abnormal and good and evil. Among the guests on *The Tonight Show* being watched by Showalter and Grimsrud and their whores is Steve Boutsikaros of the San Diego Zoo. This too is appropriate, since the kidnappers are staying in the Blue Ox Motel. Elsewhere in the film, Showalter is called a weasel by Shep Proudfoot, who is then called "Animal!" by the fleeing, half-naked hooker; another hooker says "Go, Bears," when Marge Gunderson asks her where she's from (White Bear Lake); her companion is wearing a sweater embroidered with cat designs; Marge asks if Lou, her deputy, "monkeyed" with the slain state trooper's prowler; Grimsrud, looking for unguent in the Lundegaards' medicine cabinet, discovers a porcelain pig; references are made to gophers and badgers as university mascots; and a close-up of one of Norm Gunderson's paintings reveals a blue-winged teal in flight over a swampy marshland.

Fargo's animal motif also embraces the penny-pinching Wade Gustafson: "Stan, I'm thinkin' we ought to offer [the kidnappers] half a million" [as opposed to the agreed-upon million].

Wade directs this remark to his accountant as if he were negotiating a business deal, never mind that his own daughter's life is at stake. Even the yes-man Stan Grossman is appalled at Wade's inhumanity: "We're not horse-trading here, Wade, we just gotta bite the bullet on this thing." But to Wade, a deal is a deal, whether it involves a horse or a human being.

This scene, which takes place in a restaurant, also recalls a fourth motif in *Fargo:* eating and appetite. The function of this motif is identical to that of the others: to lay bare the latent inhumanity of everyone, cops and criminals alike, in the film's entropic universe. When the voracious Marge Gunderson asks a colleague on the phone, "Would you happen to know a good place for lunch in the downtown area?" we are reminded of Gaear Grimsrud's, "Where is Pancakes Haus?"; when Marge says, "Now I'm hungry again," we recall Grimsrud's "I'm fuckin' hungry now, you know"; Norm Gunderson's "I'll fix ya some eggs" is counterbalanced by Showalter's "We'll stop for pancakes"; and so on.

The four interrelated motifs of *Fargo*—television, simulacra, animals, and appetite—are brilliantly forged into one in the film's final scene. Marge and Norm are lying in bed, pale faces illuminated by the television. We've been here before. The staticky image of *Nova's* bark beetle feeding its young is still fresh in our minds:

> TV Voice-Over: In the spring the larvae hatch and the cycle begins again.

And we know why Marge Gunderson is so ravenous throughout the film: she too is feeding her young. As for the blessed event—

> *Both of them are watching the TV as Norm reaches out to rest a hand on top of her stomach.*

> Norm: Two more months.

> *Marge absently rests her own hand on top of his.*

> Marge: Two more months.

In other words, *in the spring.*

It's most appropriate that *Fargo* should end in the reflected glow of a TV set, for, like Gaear Grimsrud, Carl Showalter, Wade Gustafson, and the Lundegaards, Marge and Norm Gunderson end the film partaking unwittingly of what the postmodern theorist Jean Baudrillard calls a *third order simulation.* Television is to the metonymic realms of *Fargo* what Disneyland, in Baudrillard's idiom, is to America:

> Disneyland is there to conceal the fact that it is the "real" country, all of "real" America which *is* Disneyland. . . . Disneyland is presented as imaginary in order to make us believe that the rest is real, when in fact all of Los Angeles and the America surrounding it are no longer real, but of the order of . . . simulation.

Fargo doesn't simply substitute fantasy for reality; rather, as Baudrillard goes on to claim of Disneyland, the film posits an "imaginary" (sic) that is "neither true nor false." In short, *Fargo* is a quintessentially postmodern film because the old binary logics of hero vs. villain *and* of hero vs. anti-hero simply don't apply. Death-in-life or life-in-death, it hardly matters.

CHAPTER 4

Criticisms of Postmodern Theory

Is There Room for Art and Beauty in Postmodernism?

Curtis White

Curtis White, professor of English at Illinois State University in Normal, is also the author of several works of fiction that have been categorized as "postmodern" by critics. While he does not necessarily resist this label, he also wonders what place the concepts of art and beauty have within postmodernism. He argues that postmodern critical theory has not helped to create a better understanding of the nature of art and beauty even as the postmodern artists and writers have dramatically changed the rules for the media in which they work. White claims that the "anti-essentialism" of postmodernism—loosely, the denial of validity to established "truths"—as practiced by Jacques Derrida and others makes the task of the artist a more difficult one because it removes potential criteria for evaluation. Since evaluation and reaction ("the morally unsettled relation of the work to its audience") is the central meaning of art for White, he resists the devaluing aspect of postmodernism and makes an appeal to the reader on behalf of art and beauty.

It has gotten difficult for me to say the words *art* and *beauty*. These two words—when I forget "what I'm about," as the British say, and use them—make me feel antique, precious, unhip, and not a little stupid. What will my theoretician friends in the English department think? "This poor nudnik. Where's he been for the last twenty years?" My embarrassment feels like an apology. I can feel an apology rising up from out of a wounded organ that stretches from my intestines to a hinter region of my brain. I think my spinal cord

Excerpted from *Monstrous Possibility: An Invitation to Literary Politics*, by Curtis White (Normal, IL: Dalkey Archive Press). Copyright © 1998 Curtis White. Reprinted with permission of Dalkey Archive Press.

wants to make amends. Here it comes: "I know that 'art' and 'beauty' have been deconstructed, demolished and otherwise banished from any thinking person's lexicon," I begin. I'm looking around now, hoping to see those reassuring nods that say, "Maybe he won't have to sleep all the way on the other side of the compound fence. With the wild animals. With the dogs we don't like." I get one or two such nods. I continue: "But I don't mean by 'artist' and 'beauty' what you think I mean." Sure buddy. Whatchoo say.

Now I make the truly desperate dodge (the substance abuser at the apex of a family intervention): "I don't want to be an Essentialist any more than you do."

Well, now I've said it. "He doesn't want to be an essentialist, Harriet."

In general, I am in agreement with the drift of ideas in the United States (i.e., the drift of Theory) in the last twenty years. What a little astonishes me, however, is that although the work of artists has continued unimpeded during this time, no new or more appropriate vocabulary has emerged in the place of our admittedly Romantic understanding of Art and Beauty to describe what it is that artists do. Artists have continued to do what they do, but they have done what they do in a sort of embarrassed silence. Artists have not known how to talk about what they do without either seeming to denounce themselves (never a comfortable position), or denouncing the conclusions of the last twenty years (in essence returning with a noisy curmudgeonliness to the high Aestheticism of Modernism, American Realism and the New Criticism). In short, there is no postmodern aesthetic. The postmodern knows not how to talk about its beauties. To be sure, there are accounts of postmodernism as a plundering anti-aesthetic of the pastiche, but there is no positive account of a postmodern artistic "ought." Unlike any previous generation of artists, no artist who is actually a member to the Moment can say to either peer or apprentice, "This is how it ought to be done. This makes it beautiful." But, as we know, artists are usually awkward when it comes to explaining why it is that what they do is important. . . .

There's nothing new in being an artist and being uncomfortable explaining what it is you are and do. The reason for the discomfort simply changes from period to period. Let's look at the logic behind the "artist question" (and the implied final solutions) for our own period as it applies to the conclusions of those who ought to understand art best, art's critics. The present discomfort of artists over their status as Artists and their embarrassed relation to something called Beauty are the result of at least two trends in critical thought which have, I believe, been applied to the activities of art in an extreme and very unhappy way. Criticism has fallen over backwards to avoid falling on its collective face. As Ezra Pound wrote (and who quotes Old Ez, *il miglior fabbro*, these days?), "It's easy to go to extremes, hard to stand firm in the middle."

Anti-essentialism. The exuberance with which younger American critics have embraced the philosophy of "anti-essentialism" (if there is a philosophy that one could call essentially anti-essential) has been at times chilling. Anti-essentialism was the conclusion of a complicated logic found by American critics primarily in the work of Jacques Derrida. Derrida argued (and argues) against "the metaphysics of presence," and "transcendental signifieds," and "the purveyors of Truth." Thus it has seemed easy to conclude that notions like "Beauty" or the "Artist" appeal to a Romantic, ideologically bourgeois and always and everywhere complicit (and therefore culpable) philosophies of the Real. Critics working under any one of a number of deconstruction's many mantles (especially New Historicism and Cultural Studies) have demystified and debunked (depending on whether it was a Romantic or ideological claim being made) the idea that the notion of Beauty has a transcendental or otherwise constant and enduring Being.

The consequence of this logic for those in the field (as anthropologists say) is that few of us have escaped the frightening (for the traditionalist), powerful (for the theorist), or anxious (for the artist) experience of being informed that concept X (Truth, fact, Reality, sense, knowledge, power, our dear friend Beauty, but you can fill in the blank) was an example of "essentializing" and therefore an already defeated concept, defeated before the discussion had even properly begun. This has had, however, the unfortunate consequence, to paraphrase Fredric Jameson, of dismissing from the field exactly the ideas about which one had come to argue. For example, in Marxist philosophy simple anti-essentialism has created a most intense and paralyzing incongruity. Because Marxism's historic appeals to notions like "freedom" or "exploitation" or "alienation" or "humanity" have been so thoroughly castigated as "essentialist," Marxists like Althusser and post-Althusserians like LaClau and Mouffe have found themselves in the (from my perspective) untenable position of arguing resistance to capitalism or the late-capitalist state for reasons that they cannot themselves articulate, have in fact rigorously forbidden themselves from articulating or appealing to. This has led to an ethical impoverishment of the Marxist tradition whose beggarly apotheosis is the glib and fatal thought of Jean Baudrillard.

Artists and critics presently find themselves in much the same untenable position. They can't simply assert the reality of Beauty as some sort of unearthly absolute (the Sublime) and no one seems to be able to articulate an alternative (although they exist), so artists and critics maintain the position of an officially embarrassed silence. An "Idealist Embarrassment," as Hans Robert Jauss once claimed of Marx's work.

As with the Marxist dilemma I have described, artists are left without a vocabulary to describe why they do what they do. Why make art? What is the role of art/beauty beyond endlessly self-deluded puppet of ideology or, on the other hand, politically correct proponent of obvious virtues? They are also left without a way of judging how one piece of art is better than another. Without a way of talking about what it means to be an immature, maturing and mature artist (maker of a particular kind of something). Any working artist must consider both of these things as a daily and ongoing function of his/her work. I'm doing it this way rather than that because it is "better" this way. What do you mean by "better"? Never mind. . . .

Against the abstractions of the conservative/Romantic ideology of art as essential and timeless reality (delivering the goods on eternal human verities) and against the self-defeat of knee-jerk "anti-essentialism," I would argue two things, the first of which seems to be bright in its simplicity and the second more subtle and shaded. The two are intimately related.

Point the first: Art as such is nothing more than its own very human traditions. That tradition is implicitly dialectical. It is complicit in nearly exactly the same proportion that it is subversive (which is why history, including art history, is really long). It seems to have a motor that keeps it always changing, but never changing so much or so quickly that it moves from "fish to fowl" in one moment. It is in many ways the tradition of our humanness itself (art articulates what it means for humans to be human). This is part of why our best artists have the most highly developed moral imaginations and the greatest "negative capability" (the power to imagine what it is like to be other people, maybe even especially other bad people). Art should not be presumed virtuous, nor should its role be presumed to be instruction in virtue. Art is not the province, as Dave Hickey writes in his brilliant little book *Invisible Dragons*, "of right-thinking creatures who presume to have cleansed its instrumentality with the heat of their own righteous anger and to be using its authority (as the Incredible Hulk used to say) as a 'force of good.'" Rather, art is about the morally unsettled relation of the work to its audience. The work uses its "beauties" to seduce the viewer to literally "incorporate" with the work, to take on the work's "body," to feel its pleasures. This is, needless to say, an often frightening and usually dubious process, but it is also the secret that Shakespeare's *Richard the Third* and even, God help us, Bret Easton Ellis's *American Psycho* know that the forces of artistic/political propriety don't.

To cut ourselves off from art and its "beauties" by arguing that they are "essentialist" or politically evil is to cut ourselves off from ourselves. The human project is the ongoing discussion of what it ought to mean to be human, and art is the most benevolent site for this discussion. . . .

In short, to abandon art's artfulness is to abandon human history, the tradition of the human as an ongoing and internally conflicted (dialectical) project, in the name of a cloistered desire for immediate "totality" (the world this way once and for all). Thus, we should speak of art as the most central place where we have carried on an enduring discussion of what we are and what we want to become. Good art demonstrates respect for the human world because of the painful/beautiful history that has brought us to this point, and also shows a certain contempt for that world because the image of a more "desirable" world can always be suggested. An awareness of and engagement with the formal history of a specific genre is an essential and inevitable requirement for this process.

Beauty.

First, poststructuralist thought is quite right about it. "Beauty" has no independent, enduring, unique, timeless being. It has no "presence" separate from (that is, transcending) immediate historical human contexts. So we shouldn't be interested in what it is but in what we say (and have said) it is. This corresponds roughly to what Foucault called historical "fact": the "it is said." History is not composed of facts; it is composed of what people say (especially in legal, medical, and otherwise "official" documents). In much the same way, Beauty is not a fixed quality; it is an ongoing dialogue.

Any given piece of art is always a composition of history (what has been said) and the moment (what the artist would contribute to what has been said even if that only means basically repeating what has been said (i.e., the boring)). Art has both an ideological and a utopic purpose and every "beautiful" piece of art will find a way of rendering both. This is, in part, what Derrida's concept of "closure" must mean for us. Whatever we do, we will work within the history of an ongoing (and often failing) project called "the human." This is, in Hegelian terms, a Spiritual exercise.

Something is beautiful when the artist works collaboratively with an inherited past, ingeniously reveals again that history within the work, but then—ah! the bright wings!—opens, allows that familiar world to unfold unfamiliarly as either a) the known world re-understood as desirable after all (the ideological) or b) a new world, surviving on bits and pieces of the past (all its parts are borrowed), and erupting as an alternative world we might inhabit (the utopic).

What's an example of a.? How about Gerard Manley Hopkins? He worked within the dying tradition of the rhymed and metered lyric in order to reinvent it as a wholly new music and in the process reinvent the relevance of (a similarly dying) Christian faith. He was, in Heidegger's words, working at "worlding," beautifully if conservatively.

What's an example of b.? How about the Beatles's *Sgt. Pepper's,* which works within the tradition of the rock'n'roll long-playing album in order to demolish and reinvent rock'n'roll, albums and the relation-to-the-world of nearly every teenager in the Western world circa 1967.

For me, beauty is the ah! of recognition not of the sublime, or a beyond. It is the complex recognition of the complex capturing of a specific human past and the formal rerendering of that past as a whole (or, okay, as Wallace Stevens would say, parts of a whole) world. Beauty always appears as the strange within the familiar. It convinces us to desire what it desires—

this strangeness—through the intensity of the pleasures its "beauty" offers. So beauty's chief anxiety is not the fear of being "ugly" but the horror of being "dead." As Dave Hickey puts it, the opposite of beauty is "the banality of neutral comfort." Beauty seduces us to desire what it desires: to be more "alive": feel this pleasure, this beauty, this strangeness. For beauty, the static quality of mere comfort is precisely despair. Needless to say, for the "socio-politically convinced," to desire to be more alive or more fully human is not necessarily to desire to be good. Thus Politic's desire to circumscribe what is tolerable in art.

My point is that we should no more wish to be done with the complicit/culpable renegade notions of art/beauty than we should wish to be done with the complicit/culpable renegade creations of sex. Simpleminded anti-essentialism and its provocative (if finally dull) companion the merely "socio-political" demand something no one should want: the termination of the human's discussion of its humanness with itself.

In the end, we are, as the painter Nicholas Africano likes to put it, "Still Human."

In spite of the facts.

Postmodernism Is Irrational

George Englebretsen

Rational thinking has formed the basis of Western intellectual life since the Enlightenment and has its roots even further in the past, at least as far back as the writings of Greek philosophers like Aristotle. George Englebretsen, professor of philosophy at Bishop's University in Quebec, claims that postmodernism is a flawed philosophical position because it claims to replace this established rational framework with a more vague position that allegedly provides full freedom of communication. Englebretsen links postmodern thought with so-called "New Age" beliefs, claiming that the de-emphasizing of reason and logic that he sees as inherent to postmodernism has fostered an environment in which people are willing to believe just about anything, regardless of what scientific fact tells them.

In Book Gamma of the *Metaphysics,* Aristotle considers the possibility that one might deny the universal logical constraints on rational discourse. In particular, he is concerned with those who might deny the law of noncontradiction ("A statement and its negation cannot both be true at the same time"). His conclusion is that such a speaker could not be counted on to say what he or she means (or mean what is said). And his advice to us is not to attempt conversation with such people.

THE FREEDOM OF IRRATIONALITY?

Postmodern thinkers claim to have broken the fetters of logic *(inter alia)* that have characterized the modern notion of rational discourse. The result, it is claimed, is a new freedom of communication. Rationality, in the sense of allegiance to uni-

Reprinted, with permission, from "Postmodernism and New Age Unreason," by George Englebretsen, *Skeptical Inquirer,* vol. 19, no. 3, May/June 1995.

versal logical constraints, is no longer the only, or even major, "communicative virtue." Social, psychological, political, historical considerations must all take precedence over logic. Judging the rational success of a piece of discourse (or "text") is now a matter to be dealt with by social scientists and literary critics rather than by logicians (the ones in whom moderns and premoderns had invested the task of defining rationality). Freed from the confines of logic, discourse can now become open, honest, sincere, politically sensitive, historically conditioned. Premoderns and moderns based their willingness to accept or reject a speaker's claim on their judgment of how well it seemed to fit the facts of the case and to what extent it was logically consistent with the speaker's other claims or assumptions. By contrast, postmoderns "play the believing game," accepting the speaker's claim according to the degree of sincerity the speaker exhibits. Truth and coherence are no longer allowed to bully us in our communicative efforts. Expertise and authority are no longer the possession of only an elite few. We all share expertise and authority equally. Communication, finally, is democratic. The premodern and modern informed and rational despots have been overthrown. We are *all* informed; we are *all* rational.

As a consequence of this newfound communicative democracy, none of us is in a privileged position relative to another when it comes to imparting knowledge and understanding. Anyone can teach anything to anyone else. Thus, no sin is greater in these postmodern times than the sin of "sub-dialogic discourse," i.e., monologue (lecturing, instructing, etc.) or null discourse (silence, closing conversation). As that guru of American postmodernism, Richard Rorty, has said, our only task is to "keep the conversation going." Aristotle's refusal even to converse with those who would reject the constraints of logic might well be considered now as Adam's Fall with respect to the "ethics of conversation."

ABSENCE OF TRUTH

So there is no truth. Or, to be fair, there is no Truth.

There are lots of little truths, all of which are relative to the social, psychological, historical, political, etc., contexts of their utterances. Consequently, there can be no disagreement. A says "X" while B says "Not X." But by postmodern lights they do not contradict one another. (Indeed, today [Walt] Whitman could not even contradict himself!) A says what she says as a woman, or as an oriental, or as an unemployed person, or as a mother, and so on and so on. B says what he says as a male, or as an Hispanic, or as an artist, and so on and so on. One man's (or woman's) "X" is another's "Not X," depending on who (= where, when, what gender, race, age, etc.) they are.

A new age of communicative democracy has now dawned, so the cant goes. And this new age has helped foster the New Age. Now there is a strong temptation to simply ignore nonsense, unreason, irrationality. The rationalist often, and understandably, wants to say that those who live in ignorance deserve the consequences. But the simple fact is that all of us suffer the consequences of willful stupidity. When reason is under attack, as it certainly is today, there are many victims. In particular, science and education are compromised, contorted, denigrated, denied. And when the war against reason is backed by a large cadre of articulate sophists (e.g., the postmodern philosophers and literary critics) the results are even more insidious. Postmoderns conjure a vision of science, viewed as "no more than the handmaiden of technology," according to Rorty, which is virtually evil itself. Science, from this point of view, is to blame for most of today's economic, environmental, and medical ills. Antiscience, pseudoscience, and literature constitute a new trivium. The latter is the "presiding discipline" of postmodern culture. Education, at all levels, is seen as contributing to the advance of this evil science. Moreover, the whole idea of education as it has been practiced since the Enlightenment is rejected on moral grounds. There can be no separation of teacher (master) and student (slave) when there are no universal standards of truth.

TOLERANCE OR INTOLERANCE?

Postmoderns are fond of their universal tolerance of all ideas. After all, by postmodern lights all ideas are equal (i.e., equally true). My idea that the reason [President] Clinton is having political troubles is because he committed a series of hurtful acts during one of his previous lives and your idea that his troubles are due to a complex array of personal and political factors are on a par with each other. Each deserves the same consideration. Each is to be tolerated. The irony here is that this universal tolerance for ideas (reasonable and unreasonable alike) is coupled with a disturbing intolerance for people. The philosophy that sees only "local" truths rather than universal truths not only repudiates science (the attempt to know the truth), but divides people according to their locality, according to who, where, when, what color, gender, etc., they are. The natural result of such division is an intolerance that, in the long run at least, tends to manifest itself in racism, nationalism, sexism, and the like. When my truth and your truth are different depending on the differences between us, then the differences between us cannot be ignored—they matter too much.

If a new Dark Age is about to descend upon us, as many believe, it will be the result of a variety of factors (just as with the last Dark Age). But surely one important factor will be the kind of thinking advocated by postmoderns and New Agers, the kind of thinking that scorns and abjures reason. If we are to keep away the darkness of ignorance and intolerance, philosophers, scientists, and educators who honor the universal benefits of modern science, liberal education, and rational discourse must cast light on today's advocates of nonsense wherever they are found. For, as Goethe said, humans fear reason, but they ought to fear stupidity—for reason can be hard, but stupidity can be fatal.

Postmodernism Lacks Lasting Relevance

Walter Laqueur

The years near the end of centuries and millennia tend to breed certain forms of extreme behavior. Walter Laqueur, chairman of the International Research Council of the Center for Strategic and International Studies in Washington, D.C., claims that the popularity of postmodernism in the last decades of the twentieth century is the result of such a millennial fervor and will therefore not last beyond the end of the millennium itself. Laqueur claims that postmodernism is an inherently flawed philosophy that is especially attractive to individuals looking for a radical philosophy to go with the upheaval that was expected to accompany the end of the millennium. Such a following makes it both overly extreme and unnecessarily elitist, since postmodernism in Laqueur's view presents itself as the replacement for ways of thinking that would be outmoded by widespread social turmoil. For him, postmodernism is an unsatisfactory way of viewing the world because it is limited to an exclusive audience and a relatively brief period of time. Thus, any literature resulting from such a philosophy would presumably only be of interest to a very small portion of society.

In the academic field, the fin de siècle [end of the century] mood manifests itself in the shape of postmodernism and post-structuralism, which includes deconstruction, postcolonial studies, American studies, the new historicism, cultural studies, and gender studies. This movement has generated great enthusiasm among its members and ridicule among its opponents; it is certainly fascinating to the outside observer. The term "postmodernism" has been applied to trends in painting since the 1880s and among architects since the 1940s, in a polemic against the Bauhaus [a style of architecture strongly associated with modernism]. According to [historian] Arnold Toynbee, writing in 1938, the postmodern phase in European culture began about 1875, and the German writer Rudolf Pannwitz referred to it in 1915 as the "great decadence of the radical revolution of European nihilism," a remarkable definition considering the date. In the 1960s, literary critics in the United States, such as Irving Howe and Leslie Fiedler, used the term, but it acquired its present connotation only in the early 1980s, probably following the publication of Jean-Francois Lyotard's *La condition post-moderne* [*The Postmodern Condition*] in 1979. The other French thinkers thought to be the founders of the movement did not refer to themselves as postmodernist. However, even before Lyotard's book appeared, the *New Yorker* announced (in 1975) that postmodernism was out.

An Unclear Distinction

The onlooker's task is not made easier by a lack of precision. It is by no means clear what the inherent differences are between postmodernism (or post-structuralism) and its predecessors, except that chronologically they came after. Seen in this light, postmodernism is an extreme, subjective species of modernism. As far as substance is concerned, the differences are often not obvious. Postcolonial theory, to give but one example, has little to do with events in the periods since the great and small empires dissolved. Instead, it means the belief that imperialism had, and continues to have, a negative impact on the colonial world. Thirty years ago the term "anticolonial" or "Third-World studies" might have been apposite. But with the disintegration of the Third World, mainly as the result of the economic success of the countries of the Far East and the failure of others, the term "African studies" would be more correct. However, neither North Africa nor South Africa wants to belong to this entity called the Third World, and on the other hand some academics in Canada and Australia wish their countries to be included.

A leading theoretician of postcolonial (and postmodern and gender studies), [Gayatri] Spivak, a professor of English literature of Indian origin, calls herself a "Third-World person." But few in India (or China or the Far East) follow her example. It has been the misfortune of the postcolonials to appear on the intellectual scene when even those in full sympathy with Third Worldism had admitted defeat. In the 1960s and 1970s, Gunder Frank, Samir Amin, and Immanuel Wallerstein had developed their theories about "dependence," "unequal exchange," and a "new socialist world system." In the 1990s, it was accepted that the Third World had disintegrated and that the attempt to build state socialism had failed. In retrospect, it seemed that the very attempt might have been an optical illusion—socialism had never been tried.

Scholars of gender and postimperialism studies were preoccupied with their own causes to such an extent that they had no wish to cooperate with others. They believed that gender (or racial) oppression was the most important thing in the world; hence their lack of enthusiasm for issues of class or the philosophies of the postmodernists. They strive for the solidarity of women—sisterhood—or of colored people but not for solidarity of human beings. As a result, a recent, widely discussed post-Marxist author has reached pessimistic conclusions about the feasibility of an international rainbow coalition because of the stress on divisions of gender and race. . . .

A MISGUIDED DESIRE FOR SOCIAL CHANGE

Postmodernism is mainly preoccupied with literary criticism and theory, with semiotics and narrative, with metacriticism, narratology, and theories of the grotesque. All this would be less noteworthy if those involved would confine themselves to their field of study—literature (or as they prefer: texts). But their ambitions go well beyond literature; their aim is to provide the key to a transformation of society. Following Jacques Derrida, they believe in the identity of politics and linguistic analysis: Language and literature determine the nature of society. Thus, one finds in *The Cultural Studies Reader* essays about shopping centers and advertising; a case could no doubt be made that these subjects should not be wholly left to economists and sociologists. Many postmodernists believe that philosophy and sociology are dead, or nearly dead, and that they have a right, in fact, a duty, to deal with subjects outside their profession! . . .

Outside observers might be struck by this positive, idealistic belief in the all-curative properties of literature. But this, alas, is not the case; the relationship of many postmodernist practitioners to their texts is more like that of a pathologist to a corpse. Their attitude to great literature is egalitarian, not elitist, for the reader is as important (if not more so) as the author, and for some of them the difference in importance between *Hamlet* and *Dallas* is not always obvious. In fact, at least some students of gender and postcolonialism display a positive dislike of literature, which they regard as a tool of exploitation, oppression, and discrimination. It is not so much love of great literature that inspires them as the conviction that deconstruction may provide the key to the most important questions of the age, questions of society, politics, the economy, and how to change them; they have a feeling that mankind may be on the eve of a breakthrough comparable to those of Isaac Newton, Albert Einstein, Karl Marx, or Sigmund Freud. And, as unkind critics would put it, they tend to forget that their endeavor, like their own field, is essentially parasitic, in the sense that art and literature can exist without interpretation, just as history and science can manage without a philosophy of history and science, but not vice versa. To paraphrase an old French textbook, "No text, no deconstruction."

WHERE AND WHY DID POSTMODERNISM BECOME POPULAR?

Where does the main support of postmodernism come from? How far has it spread? Why has it provoked such violent protests? Its main support came from students of English language and literature, although it has fellow travelers in geography, philosophy, anthropology, and architecture, where, however, postmodernism by necessity has a different meaning, namely a mixture of styles. Among the main body of psychologists, historians, and social scientists, it is largely unknown or considered irrelevant.

Attempts have been made in some quarters to develop new milestones on the road to a postmodern sociology and political science. Postmodernists claim (with some justice) that these professions are in a state of crisis, that theory has reached a dead end and is of interest only to fellow theoreticians. What do the postmodernists propose to revitalize the field? "Social narrative with a moral intent," which means the politicization of the field. But this is not exactly a revolutionary idea.

The main strength of postmodernism is in the United States, although it has considerable backing in Britain and some pockets in Scandinavia and the Netherlands. Outside the West, it is virtually unknown. In France, where most of the original inspiration originated, the intellectual debate takes place not in [the scholarly journal] *Tel Quel* but in journals such as *Commentaire, Esprit, Débat, La pensée politique,* and *Philosophie Politique,* which have little interest in postmodernism and do not even polemicize against it. To some extent it is a provincial phenomenon, even though Yale was its main cradle in the United States. Just as the postcolonialists endeavor to "provincialize" Europe, British provincial lecturers—who are providing most of the postmodernist action—seem to want to downgrade Cambridge, Oxford, and London, which have shown somewhat less enthusiasm. There seem to be more women than men in this movement. This may have to do with the prominent part played by feminist activists in the academic world; it could also reflect the increasing number of women in subjects such as English literature. However, there could be deeper reasons: In New Age (the other major manifestation of fin de siècle thinking, on which more below), there has also been strong representation by women, both as gurus and followers. Among the advocates and practitioners of postmodernism, there are excellent specialists on such traditional English-literature subjects as John Milton and Samuel Richardson, but few are at home in more than one period, let alone more than one culture. Some seem to imply that such familiarity may not be necessary, since, as they see it, the borders between disciplines have become blurred.

These students of English literature tend to refer to "late capitalism," but they are not experts in economic history, let alone physics, advanced mathematics, and molecular biology. Yet some of them have been writing on these topics confidently, distributing praise and blame and demanding revolutionary changes in these sciences. The earlier fin de siècle period also suggested a break with past traditions, but it had no scientific ambitions, and it was cosmopolitan rather than provincial in outlook.

Is Postmodernism Ultimately a Bad Thing?

Sometimes the impression is created that postmodernism is more a language than a theory. Everyone who knows the difference between difference (Ferdinand de Saussure) and *differance* (Derrida), between phallocentrism and phallogocentrism, who is familiar with Foucault's "space" and "power," who has heard about discourse displacement and interpellation, about binary opposition and margin, about intertextuality (Barthès), champ (Bourdieu), ideologeme, hegemony, and essentialism, about classeme and misprision, can, in principle, participate in the new Critical Theory debate. The feminists have made their own contribution with gynesis, selfsame, symbolic contract, relational interaction, mothering, and much more. The postcolonialists have given us "subaltern," "Western mathematics," "hybridity," and other terms, each with its own specific meaning. Fortunately, some of the post-movements texts carry glossaries, and there have been several encyclopedias covering the terms of contemporary literary theory.

Since the middle 1980s, postmodernism has been in slow decline; its advocates have been unable to agree on many things. Its effect outside the university, to the extent that it had one, has been the opposite of what was intended: It contributed to the conservative backlash in America. Radical policies with regard to crime led to a new upsurge of law-and-order slogans. Feminist attacks on the traditional family helped to bring about the reassertion of traditional family values. Allocations for the arts and humanities and for head-start operations were cut. The balance sheet is not encouraging.

Has the reaction against the "post-movements" been excessive? The defenders of liberal education were concerned about the onslaught of obscurantism at a time when intellectual standards were declining anyway. They were worried about the apparently successful efforts to propagate cultural and moral relativism. They were shocked by the cult of irrationalism and the attacks on science, by the idea that there are no truths, only perspectives. Whereas in the past those on the left (including Marxists) were almost blind believers in science and its progress, their successors have turned against it, partly because it is Western in origin, partly because of its elitist character in not being accessible to everyone. If it were true that there are certain objective laws in science, this would make it exceedingly difficult to press successfully the claim for African mathematics or feminist astronomy.

The critics in turn have been criticized for singling out certain particularly nonsensical statements made by radical

feminist or postcolonialist representatives. Was it really jus-
tified to see the barbarians at the gate, about to destroy all
that has been achieved for centuries in Western culture? The
critics would argue that the outcry against nihilism and destruction toward the end of the nineteenth century was concerned with individual works of art and philosophy, intellectual fashions that passed after a few years. The nihilism
of the late twentieth century, on the other hand, is bound to
have a longer life span because it has made inroads in
higher education, has become institutionalized, has changed
the curricula and affected the whole intellectual climate in
certain fields. Those who subscribe to it have tenure and will
remain in their positions for many years, they will appoint
like-minded spirits, and they are also immune to change.

Chronology

1924

"Frankfurt School" (Institute for Social Research) established in Germany.

1933

Adolf Hitler and the Nazi Party come to power in Germany; Frankfurt School critics go into exile.

1934

Federico de Onís uses the term *postmodernismo* to describe a movement within Spanish poetry.

1939

Flann O'Brien publishes *At Swim-Two-Birds*.

1940

Frankfurt School member Walter Benjamin commits suicide.

1944

Max Horkheimer and Theodor Adorno publish *Dialectic of Enlightenment*.

1945

United States explodes atomic bombs over Hiroshima and Nagasaki, Japan; Jorge Luis Borges publishes *Ficciones*.

1946

Winston Churchill gives "Iron Curtain" speech.

1947

Horkheimer publishes *Eclipse of Reason*.

1949

Soviet Union tests its first atomic bomb; People's Republic of China established; John Hawkes publishes *The Cannibal;* George Orwell publishes *Nineteen Eighty-Four*.

1952

United States successfully tests hydrogen bomb; Samuel Beckett's *Waiting for Godot* first performed; Ralph Ellison publishes *Invisible Man;* Kurt Vonnegut Jr. publishes *Player Piano.*

1953

House Un-American Activities Committee (HUAC), led by Senator Joseph McCarthy, begins investigating suspected communists in government and arts; Julius and Ethel Rosenberg executed as Soviet spies.

1954

William Golding publishes *Lord of the Flies;* historian Arnold Toynbee uses the term "post-modern" in *A Study of History.*

1955

Benjamin's *Illuminations* published posthumously in English; William Gaddis publishes *The Recognitions;* Vladimir Nabokov publishes *Lolita.*

1956

Allen Ginsberg publishes his poem *Howl.*

1957

Soviet Union launches Sputnik; Roland Barthes publishes *Mythologies;* Jack Kerouac publishes *On the Road.*

1958

Beckett's *Endgame* first performed.

1959

William S. Burroughs's *Naked Lunch* published in Paris; Vonnegut publishes *The Sirens of Titan.*

1960

John Barth publishes *The Sot-Weed Factor.*

1961

Michel Foucault publishes *Madness and Civilization;* Joseph Heller publishes *Catch-22;* Vonnegut publishes *Mother Night.*

1962

United States and Soviet Union come close to nuclear conflict during Cuban missile crisis; Grove Press attempts to publish Burroughs's *Naked Lunch* in the United States, spawning the nation's last major censorship trial for a work of literature; John Ashbery publishes *The Tennis Court Oath;* Nabokov publishes *Pale Fire;* Ken Kesey publishes *One Flew over the Cuckoo's Nest;* Edward Albee's *Who's Afraid of Virginia Woolf?* performed for first time; Anthony Burgess publishes *A Clockwork Orange.*

1963

Thomas Pynchon publishes *V;* Vonnegut publishes *Cat's Cradle;* Stanley Kubrick's *Dr. Strangelove* released.

1964

Donald Barthelme publishes *Come Back, Dr. Caligari;* Marshall McLuhan publishes *Understanding Media;* Susan Sontag publishes "Against Interpretation."

1965

Italo Calvino publishes *Cosmicomics;* Truman Capote publishes *In Cold Blood;* LeRoi Jones publishes *The System of Dante's Hell;* Alain Robbe-Grillet publishes *For a New Novel: Essays on Fiction.*

1966

Naked Lunch first published in United States; Barth publishes *Giles Goat-Boy;* Pynchon publishes *The Crying of Lot 49.*

1967

Barth publishes "The Literature of Exhaustion"; Barthelme publishes *Snow White;* Richard Brautigan publishes *Trout Fishing in America;* Angela Carter publishes *The Magic Toyshop;* Jacques Derrida publishes *Of Grammatology;* Gabriel Garcia Marquez publishes *One Hundred Years of Solitude;* Norman Mailer publishes *Why Are We in Vietnam?;* Robert Scholes publishes *The Fabulators.*

1968

Barth publishes *Lost in the Funhouse;* Philip K. Dick publishes *Do Androids Dream of Electric Sheep?;* William Gass publishes *In the Heart of the Heart of the Country;* Mailer publishes *The Armies of the Night;* Tom Wolfe publishes *The Electric Kool-Aid Acid Test;* Kubrick's *2001: A Space Odyssey* released.

1969

J.G. Ballard publishes *The Atrocity Exhibition;* Ursula K. Le Guin publishes *The Left Hand of Darkness;* Joyce Carol Oates publishes *Them;* Ishmael Reed publishes *Yellow Back Radio Broke-Down;* Philip Roth publishes *Portnoy's Complaint;* Ronald Sukenick publishes *The Death of the Novel and Other Stories;* Vonnegut publishes *Slaughterhouse-Five;* Dennis Hopper's *Easy Rider* released.

1970

Barthelme publishes *City Life;* Barthes publishes *S/Z;* Foucault publishes *The Order of Things: An Archaeology of the Human Sciences.*

1971

Ihab Hassan publishes *The Dismemberment of Orpheus: Toward a Postmodern Literature;* Walker Percy publishes *Love in the Ruins;* Sylvia Plath's *The Bell Jar* published in United States; Tony Tanner publishes *City of Words;* Hunter S. Thompson publishes *Fear and Loathing in Las Vegas;* Kubrick's *A Clockwork Orange* released.

1972

Barth publishes *Chimera;* Don DeLillo publishes *End Zone;* Reed publishes *Mumbo Jumbo.*

1973

Raymond Federman publishes "Surfiction"; Erica Jong publishes *Fear of Flying;* Pynchon publishes *Gravity's Rainbow;* Vonnegut publishes *Breakfast of Champions.*

1974

Heller publishes *Something Happened;* Robert Stone publishes *Dog Soldiers.*

1975

E.L. Doctorow publishes *Ragtime;* Gaddis publishes *JR;* Hassan publishes *Paracriticisms: Seven Speculations of the Times.*

1976

Reed publishes *Flight to Canada.*

1977

Robert Coover publishes *The Public Burning;* George Lucas's *Star Wars* released; Nabokov dies.

1978

Hayden White publishes *Tropics of Discourse: Essays in Cultural Criticism;* John Irving publishes *The World According to Garp.*

1979

Barth publishes *LETTERS* and "The Literature of Replenishment"; Calvino publishes *If on a winter's night a traveler;* Foucault publishes *Discipline and Punish;* Jean-François Lyotard publishes *The Postmodern Condition: A Report on Knowledge;* Gilbert Sorrentino publishes *Mulligan Stew.*

1980

Umberto Eco publishes *The Name of the Rose;* Russell Hoban publishes *Riddley Walker;* Julia Kristeva publishes *Desire in Language;* Barthes dies.

1981

MTV premieres; Jean Baudrillard publishes *Simulacra and Simulation;* Salman Rushdie publishes *Midnight's Children.*

1982

Kathy Acker publishes *Great Expectations;* Ridley Scott's *Blade Runner* released.

1983

Gilles Deleuze and Félix Guattari publish *Anti-Oedipus: Capitalism and Schizophrenia;* Terry Eagleton publishes *Literary Theory: An Introduction;* Hal Foster publishes *The Anti-Aesthetic: Essays on Postmodern Culture;* Fredric Jameson publishes *Postmodernism and Consumer Society;* Graham Swift publishes *Waterland.*

1984

Carter publishes *Nights at the Circus;* William Gibson publishes *Neuromancer;* Jay McInerney publishes *Bright Lights, Big City;* Tom Robbins publishes *Jitterbug Perfume;* Brautigan commits suicide; Foucault dies.

1985

Paul Auster publishes *City of Glass;* DeLillo publishes *White Noise;* Bret Easton Ellis publishes *Less than Zero;* Gaddis publishes *Carpenter's Gothic;* Calvin dies.

1986

Margaret Atwood publishes *The Handmaid's Tale;* Tama Janowitz publishes *Slaves of New York;* Charles Jencks publishes *What Is Postmodernism?;* Art Spiegelman publishes *Maus;* Borges dies.

1987

Hassan publishes "Toward a Concept of Postmodernism"; Maxine Hong Kingston publishes *Tripmaster Monkey: His Fake Book;* Brian McHale publishes *Postmodern Fiction;* Toni Morrison publishes *Beloved;* Jeanette Winterson publishes *The Passion.*

1988

Acker publishes *Empire of the Senseless;* DeLillo publishes *Libra;* Linda Hutcheon publishes *A Poetics of Postmodernism;* Milorad Pavic publishes *Dictionary of the Khazars;* Rushdie publishes *The Satanic Verses;* Bruce Sterling publishes *Islands in the Net.*

1989

Eco publishes *Foucault's Pendulum;* Barthelme dies.

1990

Jameson publishes *Postmodernism, or the Cultural Logic of Late Capitalism;* Pynchon publishes *Vineland.*

1991

Barth publishes *The Last Voyage of Somebody the Sailor;* Ellis publishes *American Psycho;* Donna Haraway publishes "A Cyborg Manifesto"; Douglas Coupland publishes *Generation X;* DeLillo publishes *Mao II.*

1992

McHale publishes *Constructing Postmodernism;* Neal Stephenson publishes *Snow Crash;* Tony Kushner's *Angels in America* first performed; Angela Carter dies.

1993

Irvine Welsh publishes *Trainspotting.*

1994

Eco publishes *The Island of the Day Before;* Hutcheon publishes *Irony's Edge: The Theory and Politics of Irony;* Quentin Tarantino's *Pulp Fiction* released.

1995

O.J. Simpson trial takes place; Gass publishes *The Tunnel.*

1996

Rushdie publishes *The Moor's Last Sigh;* David Foster Wallace publishes *Infinite Jest;* Joel and Ethan Coen's *Fargo* released; Alan Sokal publishes hoax article in *Social Text.*

1997

DeLillo publishes *Underworld;* Pynchon publishes *Mason & Dixon;* Acker dies.

1998

Curtis White publishes *Memories of My Father Watching T.V.*

1999

Ellis publishes *Glamorama;* Rushdie publishes *The Ground Beneath Her Feet;* Stephenson publishes *Cryptonomicon;* Heller dies; Kubrick dies.

2000

Atwood publishes *The Blind Assassin.*

FOR FURTHER RESEARCH

No succinct bibliography of as broad a category of literature as postmodernism can hope to encompass its full range. Thus, the list below is by no means exhaustive; instead, it should be seen (along with the works discussed at length in the articles within this book) as a representative sampling of some of the more accessible works that are considered relatively central to the ever-shifting idea of postmodernism.

FICTION

Kathy Acker, *Empire of the Senseless*. New York: Grove, 1990.

Margaret Atwood, *The Handmaid's Tale*. New York: Anchor, 1998.

John Barth, *Lost in the Funhouse: Fiction for Print, Tape, Live Voice*. New York: Anchor, 1998.

Jorge Luis Borges, *Labyrinths: Selected Stories and Other Writings*. New York: Norton, 1988.

Richard Brautigan, *Trout Fishing in America, The Pill Versus the Springhill Mine Disaster,* and *In Watermelon Sugar*. Boston: Houghton Mifflin, 1989.

William S. Burroughs, *Naked Lunch*. New York: Grove, 1992.

Italo Calvino, *Cosmicomics*. San Diego: Harcourt Brace, 1981.

Douglas Coupland, *Generation X: Tales for an Accelerated Culture*. New York: St. Martin's Press, 1992.

Don DeLillo, *White Noise*. Viking Critical Library. New York: Viking, 1998.

Bret Easton Ellis, *Less than Zero*. New York: Vintage, 1998.

William Gibson, *Neuromancer*. New York: Ace, 1995.

Gabriel Garcia Marquez, *One Hundred Years of Solitude*. New York: Harper Perennial, 1998.

Joyce Carol Oates, *Them*. New York: Fawcett, 1996.

Cynthia Ozick, *The Puttermesser Papers.* New York: Knopf, 1998.

Ishmael Reed, *Flight to Canada.* New York: Scribner, 1998.

Tom Robbins, *Jitterbug Perfume.* New York: Bantam, 1990.

Salman Rushdie, *Midnight's Children.* New York: Penguin, 1991.

Neal Stephenson, *Snow Crash.* New York: Bantam Doubleday, 1998.

Kurt Vonnegut Jr., *Cat's Cradle.* New York: Delta, 1998.

THEORY AND CRITICISM

Andrew Arato and Eike Gebhardt, *The Essential Frankfurt School Reader.* New York: Continuum, 1982.

Roland Barthes, *Mythologies.* New York: Noonday, 1973.

Jean Baudrillard, *Simulacra and Simulation (The Body, in Theory: Histories of Cultural Materialism).* Ann Arbor: University of Michigan Press, 1995.

Jacques Derrida, *Of Grammatology.* Baltimore: Johns Hopkins University Press, 1998.

Terry Eagleton, *Literary Theory: An Introduction.* Minneapolis: University of Minnesota Press, 1996.

Michel Foucault, *The Foucault Reader.* Ed. Paul Rabinow. New York: Random House, 1984.

Linda Hutcheon, *The Politics of Postmodernism.* London: Routledge, Kegan and Paul, 1989.

Fredric Jameson, *Postmodernism, or, the Cultural Logic of Late Capitalism.* Durham, NC: Duke University Press, 1992.

Jean-François Lyotard, *The Postmodern Condition: A Report on Knowledge.* Minneapolis: University of Minnesota Press, 1985.

John McGowan, *Postmodernism and Its Critics.* Ithaca, NY: Cornell University Press, 1991.

Brian McHale, *Postmodernist Fiction.* London: Routledge, 1987.

Curtis White, *Monstrous Possibility: An Invitation to Literary Politics.* Normal, IL: Dalkey Archive Press, 1998.

Hayden White, *Tropics of Discourse: Essays in Cultural Criticism.* Baltimore: Johns Hopkins University Press, 1985.

INDEX